Slave Escapes & the

UNDERGROUND

RAILROAD

in

NORTH CAROLINA

Slave Escapes & the

UNDERGROUND

RAILROAD

in

NORTH CAROLINA

Steve M. Miller & J. Timothy Allen

THE
History
PRESS

Published by The History Press
Charleston, SC
www.historypress.net

Cover image: *The Underground Railroad*, by Charles T. Webber, 1893. *Cincinnati Art Museum.*

First published 2016

Manufactured in the United States

ISBN 978.1.46711.785.2

Library of Congress Control Number: 2016930884

CONTENTS

ACKNOWLEDGEMENTS

W e would like to express our sincere thanks to Banks Smither, our editor, for his initial interest in this project and for his enthusiasm throughout the process. Many people have helped us in this journey, but the following were especially important in helping us to locate sources. Elise Allison, archivist, Greensboro Historical Museum; Gwen Gosney Erickson, archivist, Friends Historical Collection, Guilford College; the staff at Carteret County Public Library, Beaufort, North Carolina; the staff of the Special Collections and Archives, New Hanover Public Library; Charles Boyette, Historical Edenton; Shawn M. Rogers, director, Mendenhall Plantation; Marian Inabinett, curator of collections, High Point Museum; Matt Karkutt, consultant, Louis Round Wilson Special Collections Library, the University of North Carolina at Chapel Hill; Marsha Haithcock, director, and Rachel Kuehl, Randolph Room, Randolph Public Library, Asheboro, North Carolina; Kim Andersen and Matt Waner, Audio Visual Materials Unit, Special Collections Section, State Archives of North Carolina, Department of Natural and Cultural Resources; Lee C. Miller; Mario Ramos; and Brent S. Hayes.

Thou shalt not deliver unto his master the servant which is escaped from his master unto thee: he shall dwell with thee, even among you, in that place which he shall choose, in one of thy gates, where it liketh him best: thou shalt not oppress him.

Deuteronomy 23:15–16

INTRODUCTION

This book initially was to be about the Underground Railroad in North Carolina, but like fugitive slaves who had to backtrack and then go a different route, it became a book about runaways, slave escapes and the Underground Railroad in the Old North State. One would think these are the same things, but in fact, they can be quite distinct.

Slaves often escaped from plantations in the South. In fact, it was a common occurrence and even expected by many plantation owners. Most slaves returned after a brief respite from the harsh realities of their lives, having hid in swamps, woods and other nearby plantations or in the slave cabins of friends and family or the homes of free blacks. Running away was often a means of "controlling" the master or the overseer. It made a statement of sorts: you can beat me or overwork me, but I can retaliate by making you lose manpower and therefore income. For some, it was a brief vacation, and the respite was worth the pain that was endured after coming back home. For others, it was about family. Some ran off to be with their spouses who were enslaved on other plantations or were free. Many wanted to see children or parents. Again, the draw of family, easing the aches of days and years of divided families, was more than worth the price paid on their backs for leaving the plantation. For a few, it was a game, and sometimes the master played along; other times the retribution was anything but funny. In the end, however, it should be noted that the desire for the promise of "life, liberty and the pursuit of happiness" was the overwhelming sentiment and drive.

Many slaves ran away to a more sympathetic farmer's home, hoping to convince him that their current owner was too cruel. Relying on the system of plantation paternalism, whereby southern gentlemen were respected by their local and regional reputation, they hoped that one plantation owner could soothe the tensions, calm the beatings or unfair treatment and pave a way back home to a better life around the big house.

Many were captured, having been run down by vicious hunting dogs, sheriffs and patrols mostly made up of lower-class whites looking for easy money to supplement their poverty; most fugitives were then beaten and whipped back into submission. Some were captured by dishonest sorts—in actuality, stolen—and sold to the more terrifying Deep South, where they would be most likely worked or beaten to death. A few were welcomed back to the plantation with nominal punishments and occasionally scolded with a rather benign, "Don't do that again."

Eugene Genovese points out that many of these methods were intentional, planned and plotted by slaves who had "found an effective but dangerous method for reducing, if not eliminating, punishment." In essence, running away was a form of social control in a system of slavery that otherwise placed the slaves out of control of their lives.[1]

But some escaped. In North Carolina, they might head down east to the coast or west to Tennessee. A few aimed south, while others tramped northward. Some relied on the sympathetic Quakers or other religious groups for haven and help. Oddly, many simply wanted to go back to their previous plantations, perhaps because they were treated better, because loved ones were still there or even because of respect for their previous master. For example, some, having been purchased from coastal cities and used to the waterman's freer life, preferred that sort of servitude to working the rows of planters far inland. For others, it did not matter where they went as long as it was away from the pain and humiliation of where they had been.

Many headed for territory that only existed in the maps of their memories, having put together a pathway to freedom that was based on hearsay, conversations and anecdotes. Guided only by the North Star, they traveled through brush and hills, swamp and river, living on whatever they could find to eat and prayers for success. "Jordan River" lay north, somewhere. Others knew it as the Ohio River. Beyond that was "Canaan Land"—freedom. Others sought the help of local sympathizers, white and black, and were hidden out of sight in woods or in haystacks until the initial danger of capture was over and then were scurried off to the North. These were part of what could be called the Underground Railroad. Most, however, headed east to the swamps and coast of North Carolina, where their own brethren took them into safety and then ferreted them off to freedom. So runaways, escapees and the Underground Railroad are often distinct yet also connected.

Much of the evidence for runaways and escapees is anecdotal. For example, grandfathers and great-great-aunts passed down the stories to wide-eyed children. This is born out in a collection of essays written by young scholars in Greensboro, North Carolina. In 1932, sixth- and seventh-grade students of Mr. Abraham Peeler at Jonesboro Elementary School were given a project: interview someone from your family—parent, grandparent or other relative—about their days in slavery. This oral history project captured brief snippets of how life was for slaves. It is difficult to determine how many of those interviewed were from North Carolina, but we can assume that, of the reminiscences collected, most are genuine in one aspect or another to the Tarheel State.[2]

Young Melvin Burnett recorded that slaves who tried to run away could be killed by hanging. Vance Daye wrote down his mother's memories of her great-grandfather who "ran away one time and they could not catch him so they shot him in the leg but it did not kill him. So the man that he stayed with took care of him and he got well and he did not die. So they worked him a long time and he got bad off sick and they sold him." In an interview with "another lady," Daye found out that some slaves were often treated worse than the master's dogs, sometimes even living in the dogs' houses. Because of that, "some of the colored people fled away into the wilderness and died because they did not want to be treated like a dog." Others were found and killed.

Otis Hawkins relates one slave escape that is interesting. His great-great-grandmother was sold by her present master, "Moss Tom," as she called him, to a slave trader who proved quite cruel, so she escaped *back* to her previous master. Blondine Taylor listened to a Mrs. Johnson who recalled that even after Abraham Lincoln's Emancipation Proclamation was read, some slaves escaped and were hunted down with bloodhounds. Carl Timmons's mother also remembered that bloodhounds were used to track down runaways. But were they running away or were they slipping off to a secret rendezvous with a young lady or man? How would the master know the difference if a slave was caught and lied that he was just trying to meet a girl "somewhere good," as Irving Wallace records it? It apparently did not matter, according to Wallace. For either infraction, "if any master even found them that would be a killing."

Young Willie Mae Watkins relates a story about her grandfather that indicates some slaves who ran away were successful. The story is a bit confusing, but it is worth reading in full:

> *When my grandfather was in slavery…One day he was feeling good, the white people sent him out to work on a farm to work by himself, thought they could trust him, when he went he ran away. Some how he got back to America but he didn't no [sic] his people but he remembered his old home place and came back there. The place had changed and he didn't know his own people and he had forgotten them and their names until he got back to Greensboro…He was glad to return back to the United States of America.*

One wonders what took place in this man's life. Where did he run off to? Did he hop a ship and cross the seas? For how long? Did he actually leave the nation, only to return to Greensboro years later to people he did not know or even recognize? We will never know the full story.

The Underground Railroad is drawing a lot of attention these days. For example, a new initiative by the National Park Service is verifying and mapping out sites all over the nation. Locally, this might mean new tourism dollars for small towns and communities that need every dollar they can generate. Find an Underground Railroad site, and people will come and visit. Two recent news items demonstrate the issues involved.

There was excitement in the town of Weldon, North Carolina, in 2013 when a tunnel was discovered beneath a downtown store. According to a story in the local newspaper, the current owner of Freid's Store, Betty West, says a three- to five-foot-wide tunnel was found under the building. A ten-foot by ten-foot brick structure (other underground structures in the city are terra cotta) is over the tunnel, but flooding in the basement has prevented further research. Based on local lore, West believes the tunnel was part of the Underground Railroad. One family from Florida in search of Underground Railroad locations has already been to the site to explore. "I hope it will be some kind of draw for Weldon," West is quoted as saying. Small towns can profit big if such historic sites are located, verified, advertised and promoted.

The problem is that the hope does not fit the facts, as journalist Della Rose acknowledges. The city of Weldon has pointed out that, according to records, the building was constructed *after* the Civil War, thus it would seem the point is moot. Indeed, old maps indicate that the building was erected over an existing waterway. The tunnel in question, according to city engineers, was a drain off of the old train turntable. Still, Mrs. West is not giving up. Such is the power of the Underground Railroad mythos.[3]

In 2014, the folks of Halifax County dedicated the Roanoke Canal Museum and Trail. North Carolina African-American heritage director Michelle Lanier performed research during investigations of the site in 2013 and then gave the celebratory address. Museum director Rodney Pierce had heard of the Underground Railroad in Halifax County when he was growing up. Lanier's research helped to verify the stories into facts.

Or did it? When we read the story carefully, we see some holes. The museum centers on the Roanoke Canal, and part of the history of this canal includes stories of the Underground Railroad, as do many locations in the eastern and maritime sections of North Carolina. As Pierce says:

> *The majority of the labor on the canal was done by slaves, and the majority of the drivers of the bateaux, the boats used on the canal, were driven by slaves, so it's all connected. The only thing we don't have is something, whether through word of mouth or tangible, that actually connects the Roanoke Canal to the Underground Railroad, but we're working on it, and Ms. Lanier's lecture is a step in the right direction.*

There is quite a bit of speculation in this news story. Tangible evidence, as noted by Pierce, is still lacking. Research continues. In the meantime, ghosts of the Underground Railroad, visual and aural, still travel about the canal.[4]

We, too, have been caught up in the Underground Railroad fever. In 1997, Tim Allen moved to Snow Camp, North Carolina. This small Piedmont community was settled by Quakers in 1749, and while some Quakers in the area owned slaves, by the early 1800s, Quakers in the new nation, including those in Snow Camp, were renouncing slavery and becoming involved in what would soon be called the Underground Railroad. Cane Creek Friends Meeting in Snow Camp helped fugitive slaves find freedom; at least one member of nearby Spring Friends Meeting also was part of the freedom movement, although it was not anything like what is commonly called the Underground Railroad. Slaves would hide in Snow Camp on their journey to Greensboro, where more supporters waited to help.

Just next door to Tim's house once stood Freedom's Hill Wesleyan Church. This congregation started in protest to the local Methodists who defended the practice of slavery. The white clapboard church, originally constructed in 1847, no longer stands in Snow Camp: now it sits, fully restored, on the beautiful campus of Southern Wesleyan University, in Central North

Freedom's Hill Wesleyan Church. *Courtesy of Myrtle Phillips.*

Carolina. But, its legacy lives on in Snow Camp because, according to local lore, it, too, was part of the Underground Railroad.

Along with this, at least two houses in Snow Camp were part of the Underground Railroad as well. One, called the Kirkman House, was empty during the slavery years, but local legend suggests that slaves hid in the house during the day. Clothes and food were stocked in the house for runaways. Just a few hundred yards away, another house had a separate kitchen structure just across the road from Cane Creek Meeting. In this kitchen was a potato cellar that was covered by four numbered floorboards and then a rug. The descendants of the owners recall that the family hid runaways there, as well as potatoes. All of these stories are enumerated in Tim Allen's book *Snow Camp, North Carolina*, published by The History Press in 2013. As this book goes to publication, the community of Snow Camp is working on the paperwork to be recognized as a legitimate Underground Railroad site.

So with all of this lore about Quakers and the Underground Railroad in North Carolina, it was just a matter of time before Tim began to search in earnest for more stories on the Underground Railroad in the Tarheel State. When he looked for modern books on the subject, he discovered that there were plenty on the Underground Railroad in the North: indeed, The History Press had published at least four books on the topic. But books on the Underground Railroad in the South, such as Stephen B. Weeks's *Southern Quakers and Slavery*, are out of print and thus difficult to find for the average reader. The volume by Steven B. Weeks had just been republished, but it would not contain any of the recent findings that scholars had published. Then we began to notice something. The authors of the more recent *A History of African Americans in North Carolina* do not even mention the Underground Railroad. Imminent authority Eugene Genovese's seminal and exhaustive work on slavery *Roll, Jordan, Roll* mentions the Underground Railroad once, and that reference is from a work by W.E.B. Du Bois. Respected North Carolina historian William Powell refers to the Underground Railroad only three times in his well-known history of the Tar Heel State, *North Carolina Through Four Centuries*. Milton Ready, in his textbook on North Carolina history, does not mention the Underground Railroad at all. The Underground Railroad is mentioned several times in a chapter of David Cecelski's excellent work,

Kitchen in Snow Camp, constructed circa 1843, where runaways were hidden under the floor. *Courtesy of Tim Allen.*

The Waterman's Song, about slavery in the maritime areas of North Carolina. With all the oral lore about the Underground Railroad in North Carolina, one would think that the histories would be full of stories corroborating the clandestine means of escape.

People in the state talk a lot about the Underground Railroad as if it were commonplace. So why the disparity between oral histories and local lore and respected published works on slavery and North Carolina history? Certainly a book on the Underground Railroad in North Carolina was long overdue if for no other reason than to clarify this mystery. Still, with these stories in mind we need to be careful as we investigate the Underground Railroad in North Carolina.[5]

So Tim called upon a former student, Steve, and asked if he was interested in working on the project. Steve was excited and eager to work on his first book. The project was larger than either one of us could have successfully finished. But as we began our research, one difficulty arose: what was the Underground Railroad *in North Carolina*?

Mention the "Underground Railroad" in a discussion and suddenly a whole collage of interpretations and images arises. The excellent 1984 article in *National Geographic* by Charles L. Blockson describes the Underground Railroad that we are familiar with.[6] Most can recall lessons from school projects that featured Harriet Tubman and slave quilt designs and code signals from old Negro spirituals. Others might include more specific images and details from various regions of the nation: safe houses; rooms with secret compartments and wagons with false bottoms; potato cellars "hidden" underneath rugs placed over floorboards; clandestine meetings in the dark of winter nights; finding nails on the northern, moss-covered sides of old trees; and brutal beatings of slaves caught trying to escape. Whispers of secret greetings, specific knocks on doors and hoot owl calls in the night are often heard at lectures in local libraries or civic groups. A few might even know of local lore and legends involving the railroad in their area. Even coded letters are referred to, like the following: "By tomorrow evening's mail you will receive two volumes of the 'Irrepressible Conflict' bound in black. After perusal, please forward, and oblige."[7]

Old damp, dark cellars; hidden spaces behind chimneys and secret compartments in crumbling log houses; and long tunnels from a mansion to the nearby river are often discussed. But as we will see in the following pages, for North Carolina, are these legitimate indicators of Underground Railroad activities or just oddities in local architecture? For example, in Jamestown, North Carolina, there is the Richard Mendenhall Plantation, which features the house of the Quaker tanner that served as a gathering place for locals and a watering hole for travelers in the 1800s. In the barn of the plantation is a wagon with a false bottom that was used to transport slaves in some way. This issue is not in question. Because of this one item, however, many people often assume that Richard Mendenhall was an active Quaker whose house was part of the Underground Railroad. Indeed, it is taken as fact in one scholarly article.[8] The story becomes even more enticing when the topic of a "dead man's door" in the plantation is brought up. This may or may not be the case. As director of Mendenhall Plantation Shawn M. Rogers explains in a video, it can't be proven slaves were hidden on the plantation. But, Rogers goes on to note, not far from the plantation was another Quaker plantation with a similar door that did harbor fugitive slaves. So was Mendenhall Plantation a safe place for runaway slaves? Have the oral stories passed down through the years conflated the two plantations? Maybe. Maybe not.[9]

Along with this, there has been a lot of what might be called wishful thinking about aspects of the Underground Railroad. For years, folklore related that quilts were used as direction signals and information boards for runaways heading north. Thus, it was time for celebration when Jacqueline Tobin and Raymond Dobard published their fascinating book, *Hidden in Plain View: A Secret Story of Quilts and the Underground Railroad*. It is the account of African American quilter Ozella McDaniel Williams, who related a story passed down through generations of her family of how quilts were used to guide fugitive slaves to freedom. But, as African American Giles Wright, who is the director of the New Jersey Historical Commission's Afro American History Program, notes in a scathing critique delivered on June 4, 2001, to the Camden County, New Jersey Historical Society, the whole book is yet another modern myth about the Underground Railroad. At the very most, it refers only to an obscure, local tradition that centers around Charleston, South Carolina.[10] However, most schoolteachers apparently do not know this because the book is regularly listed as a source for projects on the Underground Railroad.

Another possible flight of fancy might be the current obsession with Negro spirituals and the Underground Railroad. Tim found one example of this at a folk festival on Ocracoke Island. One noted singer and storyteller was overheard relating how specific "code" words in certain spirituals gave directions and information to fleeing slaves. Slave communities would sing these songs in the fields or at night while fugitives lay in hiding nearby. But was this really the case? In the *New Century Hymnal*, published by the United

Church of Christ, the African American spiritual "Keep Your Lamps Trimmed and Burning" has the following historical note: "This spiritual is possibly one of the code songs in which to keep one's lamp 'trimmed and burning' could have meant keeping a lookout for a conductor of the underground railroad, such as Harriet Tubman." Interestingly, in Catherine Clinton's biography of Tubman, there is no mention of spirituals nor music used in her work on the Underground Railroad. Not to mention that a burning lamp would draw attention to the hiding slave or to bounty hunters looking for a safe house. Blockson suggests Harriet Tubman "doubtless" sang such coded spirituals as "Steal Away to Jesus" and "Wade in the Water." There is no proof of this, but Blockson goes on to note that the outspoken voice for slaves Frederick Douglass recalls that "Canaan" as sung in slave spirituals was code for Canada.[11] So maybe the spirituals were indeed part of the slaves' escape experience.

The information on the Guilford College Friends Historical Collection website provides a sober review of another spiritual, "Deep River." Was this song also a code for slaves running to freedom? Did it refer to the Deep River settlement of Quakers in the Piedmont of North Carolina and thus have some connection to their involvement in the Underground Railroad? Do the lyrics refer to places on the Underground Railroad lines? Does "over Jordan" refer to the Ohio River or just *the* or even *a* Deep River? In the historical video clip from the Library of Congress that covers "Deep River" on the Guilford College website, there is no mention of any connection to the Underground Railroad.

Questions still abound. If this and other spirituals really were part of the lore and necessities of the Underground Railroad, why haven't others—slaves or scholars from long ago—brought this up? Indeed, writing in the mid-1900s, noted African American theologian Howard Thurman explored the lines of "Deep River" and pointed out that for slaves who sang this song, "quite practically the river may have been for many the last and most formidable barrier to freedom." But Thurman does not mention the Underground Railroad in his meditation on this and other spirituals nor does he link the spiritual to any sense of slave escapes. Instead, he illuminates the spiritual significance of the river motif. The connection of "Deep River" and other spirituals to the Underground Railroad could very well be a modern invention.[12]

The Underground Railroad brings with it a haunting mystique that is blurred by the mists of time and the darkness of tales and the inherent secrecy that was necessary to protect those fleeing the peculiar institution in the South. However, what we found in our investigation is that these details are not very prominent in North Carolina stories of slave escapes. Indeed, if we define the Underground Railroad this closely, it could be argued that the Underground Railroad did not even exist in North Carolina. But the northern part of the Carolina colony was no stranger to escaping slaves and even servants, white and black.

Long before the Underground Railroad was constructed, North Carolina had a reputation as the runaway state. While Virginia and South Carolina planters managed large plantations with numerous slaves, North Carolina was slow to develop into a slave state. The Lower Cape Fear area was home to a planter elite only after 1755. Tarheel State slave owners held few—generally less than five each—in bondage and often worked closely with them as well. Relationships were not as brutal as those between slaves and masters in South Carolina and Virginia. Thus, servants and slaves from these states often fled to the Tarheel State for freedom. The problem was so bad that in 1691, Virginia governor Francis Nicholson accused North Carolinians of providing sanctuary to runaways. North Carolina governor Walker responded in 1699 with a statute that imposed large fines for those caught providing refuge for runways.[13]

John Hope Franklin concluded, "Ante-bellum North Carolina was the scene of much movement to and from plantations by runaway slaves." While many fugitives left for the North or another Southern state, Franklin argues that most stayed in North Carolina, moving to areas where free blacks dominated, blending in with the free population. Indeed, because North Carolina was quite hospitable to freed blacks, fugitives from other states often fled to North Carolina. Part of the draw was the lax attitude toward current laws. Even Booker T. Washington was aware of the good situation in North Carolina. Franklin notes that of the eight counties in North Carolina with the highest populations of free blacks, four were on the North Carolina–Virginia border and one was on the South Carolina–North Carolina border. In early 1827, a bill was passed by the North Carolina legislature that prohibited free blacks and mulattoes from entering the state.[14]

Indeed, the largest population of fugitive slaves in the South was in the northeast portion of the state. Hidden within the imposing confines of the Great Dismal Swamp were thousands of runaways and fugitives who intermarried with Indians and whites and created villages with often complex systems of governance and economy. This was quite well-known: poet Henry Wadsworth Longfellow penned "The Slave in the Dismal Swamp," in which he described how the negro was hunted by hounds baying in the swamps.

Harriet Beecher Stowe, author of *Uncle Tom's Cabin*, wrote another book after that famous tome, *Dred: A Tale of the Great Dismal Swamp*. By the time of the American Revolution, there were also significant fugitive slave numbers in Wilmington, Edenton and New Bern.[15]

Questions, sometimes buoyed by myth and ignorance, abound when the Underground Railroad is mentioned. Was there really such an entity? Some scholars, such as Larry Gara, do not believe there was an Underground Railroad in the United States as extensive as has been described by others. Indeed, Gara argues that the very notion of an Underground Railroad might be a northern myth, invented and grown alongside the emergence of the southern myth of the Lost Cause that emerged after the Civil War.[16] Other scholars—nurtured on the necessities of facts, not hearsay—ask, "Where is the tangible proof? Show me documents that say slaves were actually hidden in this particular closet, this cellar, this hollow tree."

The story of the slave Solomon or Saul as told by Addison Coffin helps us to better understand this claim. In 1835, Solomon was sold to a slave dealer who happened through New Garden (modern-day Greensboro) and who then sold him to a plantation owner in Georgia. Wearing a heavy iron neck collar and connected to a coffle (slaves chained together), Solomon memorized the names of roads, rivers, taverns, towns and camps as he and others were dragged to the Deep South and horrible servitude. After a year or so, he planned his escape. He packed as much food as he could carry and fled north back to New Garden. Along the way, he fought off hounds that were trained to track and maim or kill escaped slaves. He hid in bramble thickets and literally fought his way back home. There were no whites who helped him back to New Garden.

Solomon was sequestered near the Coffin home until he recuperated from his wounds and famished state. Then Addison either conducted him along or placed him on the Underground Railroad to safety and freedom. The information is vague at that point in Addison Coffin's travelogue.[17] Coffin's recollections both support and yet also refute Larry Gara's claims that there was no Underground Railroad in North Carolina. Such is the mystique!

As we look at slave escapes and the Underground Railroad in North Carolina there are also some assumptions that need to be addressed. Most people believe that the Underground Railroad was only for black slaves. Addison Coffin remembers that white slaves, most likely meaning children of white owners and black female slaves, many of whom did not know anything about the possibility of freedom, were also skirted away through the Underground Railroad.[18] This provides an interesting twist to the usual

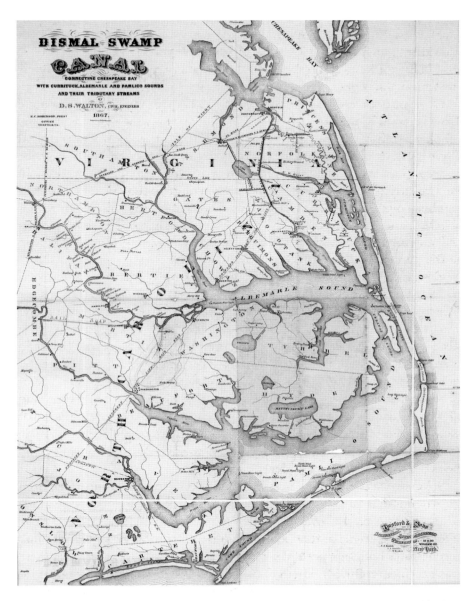

Map of the Dismal Swamp Canal. Colonies of fugitives and maroons lived deep within the confines of "The Dismal" for decades. *Wikimedia.*

understanding of the Underground Railroad. It might come as a surprise that a few Confederate soldiers in the Piedmont section of North Carolina who were deserting their ranks used the Underground Railroad to escape to the North. Likewise, Union soldiers who escaped capture by the Rebels used the Underground Railroad to flee back home. And conscientious objectors fled the slave South on the tracks of the Underground Railroad.

There was also an "Over-ground Railroad" in use. Some slaves rode in plain sight of others in wagons, on horses, on trains and on foot behind wagons. Many had been legally purchased by Quakers and then set free. Some carried "papers" that proved they were the property of legitimate white folks, and once they arrived at their destination, they were set free.

The Underground Railroad was not landlocked. Lost in the lore are the stories of crossing water as well. Many slaves crossed rivers—the most famous being the Ohio River, also known as Jordan—but other slaves crossed rivers such as the Rio Grande and Mississippi and the Atlantic Ocean to places such as Haiti and the West Indies. As we shall see, the Atlantic also served as a route to destinations like Philadelphia, Boston and New York, where escapees could establish a permanent residence or move on to Canada. In North Carolina, many slaves crossed rivers, marshes, swamps and sounds as they ran, rowed and swam for freedom.

Likewise, many believe that the organization was clandestine, secret. That may have been the case in the South, where the penalties for aiding slave escapes could be anything from being ostracized by neighbors to jail time and even death. But in numerous instances in the North, locals knew who the operators, conductors and supporters were. In 1844, the *Chicago Western Citizen* ran an advertisement for the Underground Railroad. "Superintendent" G.W. Burke publicly noted the railroad was running well. A cartoon in another paper actually gave the name of the local conductor. One man even advertised that he was the local Underground Railroad agent.[19] Locals often knew of the safe houses and routes. In the North, some Underground Railroad leaders such as Levi Coffin openly bragged to people of their exploits. In the late 1700s, it was well known that Quakers in the Perquimans County area of North Carolina were helping slaves escape.

Then there is the notion of region itself. Reading over books and articles on the Underground Railroad it is clear that it means something very tangible in the North, while in the South it is more ephemeral. There is ample documentation that houses, churches and businesses in the North were used as safe houses: there are many family histories and local oral histories that call up snippets of memories about seeing a black man in a cellar closet or a plate of food just delivered in the safety of night by the house owner. But what becomes apparent while chasing down the Underground Railroad in North Carolina is that it is less a planned, documented system and more of a catch-all phrase that might include overground trips to Ohio, secret cellars in kitchens, hidden communities in swamps, small clandestine religious groups who worked together to breach the walls of slavery one soul at a time, ship captains who risked their lives to transport a runaway and, as the Civil War neared its end, the intentional forays of Northern troops, white and black, into areas to bring slaves to freedom and even recruit them for military service. Sometimes it was something as unromantic and boring as purchasing a slave and then driving her to freedom in Ohio. And for every Harriet Jacobs and Levi Coffin in North Carolina, there were many escapes and flights based merely on hopes and hearsay that turned into freedom. One thing that becomes quite clear is that in North Carolina, the slaves overwhelmingly took the initiative and were then helped by other blacks and some whites. This quickly dispels the long-held myth that the Underground Railroad in North Carolina was run by whites who helped the hapless slaves find freedom.

Last, there is the incorrect notion that all slaves headed *north* to freedom. What of slaves in Texas who ran *south* to Mexico? According to former slave Felix Haywood, hundreds of slaves walked to the Rio Grande, where they waded and swam over to freedom.[20] Other slaves in the Deep South fled to New Orleans, where they might board a ship for England. In the Carolinas and Georgia, some slaves escaped to the Caribbean Islands. The Bahamas were also part of the picture as well. And as manumission societies organized, there was an initial effort to take slaves back to Africa. In North Carolina, slaves ran toward all the points on the compass. Not all slaves looked north for freedom. Real freedom was anywhere, in any direction, that did not mean working for the current master.

There is one myth that must be addressed immediately: that the North was quite hospitable to fleeing slaves. This notion has been perpetuated in many history books throughout the decades, perhaps part of the lasting moral punishment meted out by the North after the Civil War upon the South. The fiction that an antislavery, abolitionist North opened its arms in love to all African slaves who fled to it for freedom has been perpetuated by well-intended yet misinformed scholars and teachers for quite some time. This is curious because as early as 1898, with the publication of William Siebert's well-documented volume on the Underground Railroad, this notion is dispelled. He writes, "The truth is, the mass of the people of the free states were by no means abolitionists; they cherished an intense prejudice against the negro."[21]

Now there is more and more evidence that the North was just as responsible for slavery, and the incipient racism that grew with it, as the South. For example, while Vermont was the first state to outlaw slavery, at least one author was surprised to find out that the state was anything but welcoming to fugitive blacks.[22] The citizens of Indiana and Illinois, frightened at the large influx of both free blacks and slaves who arrived across their borders thanks in part to the efforts of many North Carolina Quakers, passed laws in 1831 and afterward forbidding masters (like North Carolina Quakers who had purchased slaves in order to give them freedom) to dump off their slaves there or prohibiting freed slaves from coming there. Pennsylvania likewise began turning away slaves in the 1830s.[23] This reluctance on the part of Northern states to receive slaves may have been the very catalyst for the Underground Railroad. It might have even played a role in North Carolina slaves running for freedom within their own state.

We believe as you read this book, you will see what became evident to the authors of this book: that the mounds of material available on slave escapes in North Carolina do not necessarily point to an organized, hierarchical Underground Railroad. Otherwise, it would not have been necessary, for example, for one soul portrayed within these pages to have hidden in an attic for seven years prior to escaping the Tarheel State. Any real, highly functioning system to aid slaves in fleeing the shackles of their masters was probably more a product of Northern port cities, like Philadelphia. Even then, it depended on the activity of the local manumission society, or vigilance committee.

The purpose of this book is to bring together many tales and bits of information about slave escapes and the Underground Railroad in North Carolina. We will tackle a few critical issues, yet overall, this book is for a general readership. We will see that definitions are hard to come by, specific proof is often elusive as it is based more on local legend than verifiable facts and that in some cases, the term Underground Railroad is actually a misnomer. In many cases, we purposely resort to hearsay, oral traditions and anecdotal local lore, knowing that while scholars may avoid these like the plague, oftentimes there are nuggets of truth in the mines of community myths.

Still, our conclusion is that there is enough evidence to suggest that there was a surreptitious "system" of people and trails and stops and safe places that can be loosely called an Underground Railroad in North Carolina.

Chapter 1

THE UNDERGROUND RAILROAD: A CONFUSING IDEA

Ask someone what the term Underground Railroad means and most people can come up with some answer like the following: it was a system of conductors and safe houses that was, in effect, for slaves to use to flee bondage in the South. Safe houses had secret rooms, and tunnels led from one house to another location. There were conductors and lines, and most slaves were helped in the dark of night. People like Harriet Tubman single-handedly saved thousands of runaways by risking their lives to lead them through the woods and clandestine trails that marked the Underground Railroad.

Look around on the Internet and more information, and even misinformation, can be located. The PBS website provides the following information on the Underground Railroad:

> *The Underground Railroad, a vast network of people who helped fugitive slaves escape to the North and to Canada, was not run by any single organization or person. Rather, it consisted of many individuals—many whites but predominently [sic] black—who knew only of the local efforts to aid fugitives and not of the overall operation. Still, it effectively moved hundreds of slaves northward each year—according to one estimate, the South lost 100,000 slaves between 1810 and 1850.*[24]

Information from the National Park Service website reiterates that the Underground Railroad was not a universal organization. "The Underground

Railroad refers to the effort—sometimes spontaneous, sometimes highly organized—to assist persons held in bondage in North America to escape from slavery."[25] This information is especially true for North Carolina.

One of the problems in discussing the Underground Railroad is that there is so much misleading and conflicting information for people to sift through. Here is one example: Alex Coffin, in his article on NCpedia.com, notes that it was a "secret system of individuals who assisted fugitive slaves in their quest for freedom before the Civil War."[26] This may have been true for the United States, but it is not entirely accurate for North Carolina. A few individual Quakers in the Piedmont worked together initially, but it was not an organized system by any means in the Tarheel State. In the coastal areas, the only verifiable systematic efforts were by Northern troops during the Civil War who made forays into slave country purposely to locate, free and recruit slaves for their cause. Otherwise, many slaves fled on their own and trusted the bits and pieces of information available locally to escape. According to Larry Gara, the few systems that were in place were in Northern cities with large free black populations—Cincinnati, Philadelphia and Wilmington, Delaware.[27] No doubt North Carolina cities such as New Bern and Wilmington with substantial free black populations were able to help fugitive slaves find freedom as well. But overall, there does not appear to be a large, *organized* Underground Railroad system in the Tarheel State.

The PBS website also points out that the term Underground Railroad was in existence from about 1830 to 1860. Then the website informs us that Vestal Coffin formed an Underground Railroad station in Guilford County, North Carolina, in 1819. This implies that the *system* was in place before it actually was. More accurately, as has been recorded, slaves escaped to the Greensboro area where Vestal Coffin lived. They hid in the dense woods near his house and sought his help because they had heard he was against slavery. Thus, he began helping slaves escape in 1819 at his home in Guilford County, and then, as the movement began to escalate, it *eventually* earned the term "Underground Railroad" because, as the website goes on to say, slaves escaped swiftly and seemingly invisibly. As all of the Coffins make explicitly clear in their writings, none of them actively sought runaways to guide to freedom.

Adding more confusion to the mix is Greensboro's Addison Coffin's (brother of Vestal Coffin and cousin of Levi Coffin) memories of the Underground Railroad. Published in 1898, Addison writes that many "entered the service of that mysterious institution in or previous to 1835."[28] As we will see, establishing any precise date of the Underground Railroad is nearly impossible.

Another issue is geography. The answer to "What is the Underground Railroad?" may literally depend on which side of the Mason-Dixon line you stand on. Seibert's work demonstrates that the overwhelming majority of the Underground Railroad activity was in the North. What of the South? One North Carolinian may have an answer that provides a unique perspective. The Quaker Levi Coffin—who grew up in what is now Greensboro, North Carolina, but later moved to Indiana in 1826, where he served as the "president" of the Underground Railroad for nearly all of his life—offers this description in his recollections.

> *I have always contended that the Underground Railroad, so called, was a Southern institution; that it had its origin in the slave States. It was, however, conducted on quite a different principle south of Mason and Dixon's line, from what it was on this* [Indiana] *side. South of the line money, in most cases, was the motive; north, we generally worked on principle. For the sake of money, people in the South would help slaves to escape and convey them across the line, and by this means, women with their children, and young girls…were enabled to reach the North. They were hidden in wagons, or stowed away in secret places on steamboats, or conducted on foot through the country, by shrewd managers who traveled at night and knew what places to avoid.*[29]

Coffin's comments demonstrate that, nationally, there was not a unified Underground Railroad and that there were at least two different philosophies in place that warranted two different systems of attack and help. Levi Coffin also reveals throughout his recollections that slaves from the South often looked toward the North Star and simply walked through thickets, fields, swamps and roads in order to reach the Ohio River and cross to freedom, where they would then seek the help of those in a more organized Underground Railroad. This anecdote, along with others offered by Coffin in his *Reminiscences*, also suggests that there was a "black" and then "white" system in place, sometimes working separately, other times together. Thus, in many cases slaves made their own routes north. This suggests that, for some slaves the system of conductors and stations and lines that many have learned about in school projects may have been more in the North once they crossed into a free state, but that, until then, fugitive slaves were on their own in North Carolina.

The Underground Railroad in the North was more organized, with societies that sewed clothes for runaways, bought shoes for them, had several different routes to the next depot and worked often in the open to get slaves ultimately to Canada and freedom, as Levi Coffin notes throughout his memoirs. Stockholders "invested" in the Underground Railroad, and their money was used to rent teams of horses, buy shoes or items of clothing and other commodities and services as needed. Books on specific locales of the Underground Railroad indicate localized pockets of houses with safe rooms, hidden spaces behind stairwells, tunnels beneath houses and churches and possibly even public signs with hidden meanings. Stories abound of children seeing black people in the cellar in the night or asking why Dad has hitched up the mules to the wagon at night or even parents strictly forbidding their children to tell anyone of the black family they saw at the door at two in the morning. Barns with compartments under the floors, mills with hidden rooms and zig-zag routes from one safe house to another, one community to another, sometimes even backtracking, were part of the lore. "Conductors," "stations" and "codes" made the journey all the more romantic and dangerous. Freed blacks were major leaders of the initial lines, but more and more whites became involved. There is an individualized complexity to the Underground Railroad that has not been fully appreciated, overshadowed by the generalized myths and legends and even misinformation that we have taught in our schools for generations.[30]

What specific routes did the Underground Railroad take? Again, this depends on whether one is talking about the North or the South. Seibert's work presents a meticulously drawn map of specific routes that he has collated from correspondence with numerous former conductors and others involved in the northern Underground Railroad operation. When we move to the South, we suddenly hit generalities. The National Park Service website offers

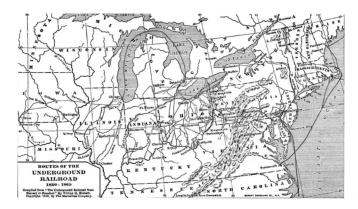

Routes of the Underground Railroad map, compiled from William Siebert's *The Underground Railroad: From Slavery to Freedom.*

a map that details the major escape routes for slaves on the Underground Railroad. Interestingly, there is a major route from South Carolina northward through the Piedmont of North Carolina that continues through Virginia to Baltimore, Wilmington, Delaware and Philadelphia. A "spur" veers right from the North Carolina Piedmont toward the Great Dismal Swamp toward northwest North Carolina and southwest Virginia.[31] We will see that there is much more to the movement of fugitive slaves in North Carolina than this map details. For example, the map ignores the work of the Coffin family in Greensboro. Many other Society of Friends members as well took slaves from Greensboro to Indiana and Ohio in the early 1800s. Also, several boats left from the port of Beaufort for Africa with cargoes of slaves that were gathered by Quakers.

Chapter 2

THE UNDERGROUND RAILROAD: BACKGROUND AND DEFINITIONS

O n April 9, 1865, Confederate general Robert E. Lee surrendered his tired, hungry and haggard Army of Northern Virginia to General Ulysses S. Grant. Later that same month, on April 26, General Joseph E. Johnston surrendered more than eighty-nine thousand troops that comprised what was left of the Confederate forces from North Carolina down through Florida. Finally, after four years of the worst bloodshed that has ever stained American soil, the Civil War was, for all practical purposes, over. More than the thunder of cannons and guns ceased when these two armies laid down their arms, however. The institution of slavery also came to an abrupt end. A system of chattel labor, supported by the Constitution of the United States and by colonial and state laws, beginning in Virginia in 1661, passed into infamous history.[32]

Long before there was a divided nation, and long before African Americans held in bondage were freed, thousands of slaves obtained freedom for themselves by various means. Sometimes slave owners granted slaves their liberty following years of service. As was the case with George Washington, there were instances when slave masters arranged for the emancipation of their slaves in their wills. Washington delayed liberation for his slaves until his wife, Martha, was deceased, saying, "Upon the decease [of] my wife, it is my will and desire th[at] all the slaves which I hold in [my] *own right* shall receive their free[dom]."[33]

Sometimes, when slaves were allowed to earn some money of their own, they would save their earnings until they had accumulated enough cash to purchase their freedom from their owner. If a former slave had a wife and family still in bondage, he also would often save his wages until he could purchase the liberty of loved ones.

One instance when a slave was allowed to purchase his manumission took place in North Carolina. Lunsford Lane was born a slave in Raleigh, North Carolina, in 1803. He was owned by Mr. Sherwood Haywood, who possessed plantations outside of the Raleigh city limits but kept slaves for the service of himself and his family in town. Haywood was a rather benevolent slave owner for the time and had allowed his slaves in Raleigh to

Lunsford Lane, former slave, circa 1879. *Courtesy of the State Archives of North Carolina.*

learn how to read and write, in spite of state laws prohibiting such actions. He also sanctioned Lane's measures toward earning money with which he planned on purchasing his freedom.

Haywood died before he and Lane could fulfill their agreement, but Haywood's widow was also willing to allow Lane to buy his liberty. Therefore, Lane set about selling his own tobacco in Fayetteville, Chapel Hill and as far away as Salisbury. It took him about eight years, but he raised $1,000. However, because of North Carolina law, he had to find a white male who was willing to buy him and then petition the court to free him.

Mr. Benjamin B. Smith was willing to buy Lunsford Lane and petition the court on his behalf. The sale was made, and good to his word, Mr. Smith applied to the court, but the court refused. Lane and Smith agreed though that Lane would accompany Smith, who was a merchant, to travel with him on his next trip north, where Lane could be granted his freedom. Therefore, one year later, in New York City, Lunsford Lane acquired his emancipation papers.[34]

Putting their trust in the hands of a white slave master did not come easily to slaves such as Lunsford Lane, and with good reason. Even following an agreement on the amount of money required to free someone, owners could—and sometimes did—renege on their promise. A friend of Lane's was promised his release upon the payment of $800. Yet, once the payment was made, the slave's owner did not petition the courts for the enslaved man's emancipation. Lane's friend ultimately ran away.[35]

Earlier, around the time the Continental Congress made the commitment to American independence, the Society of Friends, or Quakers, were committing themselves to abolition. Slaves held in bondage by Quakers were quickly being given their freedom. Further, Quakers began a process of purchasing slaves from their slave-holding neighbors, when they could, and liberating them.[36]

Another means of obtaining freedom for a bondsman was military service. During the American Revolution, slaves held in perpetual servitude actually had a choice: they could, by proclamation of the Royal Governor of Virginia, Lord Dunmore, join British forces and thereby gain their freedom. Within one week of Dunmore's proclamation in November 1775, over three hundred slaves escaped their respective plantations and managed to make their way to his ship, anchored in the Chesapeake Bay.[37]

However, there was an American option for slaves to achieve their liberty during the war as well. Often, a slave owner, rather than opting for a state's militia or serving in the Continental army himself, would send an able-bodied slave in his place, promising to free him after their service. Sadly, the promise was not always kept. Some whites would buy a slave solely for the purpose of sending them in harm's way in their stead. This was done by William Kitchen just before the Battle of Guilford Courthouse in 1781.

Kitchen deserted his post on the North Carolina line but was captured and returned to duty. At that point, Kitchen purchased a slave named Ned Griffen, described as "a man of mixed blood," from William Griffen. Ned served in the place of Kitchen for twelve months. Kitchen defaulted on his promise to free Ned Griffen, but fortunately for the slave, the General Assembly granted Griffen his freedom in 1784.[38]

For those in perpetual servitude who were not set free by their owners, were not permitted the opportunity to purchase their emancipation from their masters or were not freed following military service, the only other option was escape. How many slaves were able to make their way to a free state or Canada, no one really knows. They would sometimes wait until the dead of night and make their escape. Some would wait until they had the confidence of their masters and simply never return when sent to a neighboring plantation or town. Still others would be bold enough to abruptly walk off the plantation and hope for the best. For many slaves, one failed attempt was enough. The resulting cruel punishment wasn't worth it.

Still, for others, one brief taste of freedom wasn't sufficient. Many made their dash for freedom numerous times, despite the consequences of being captured. One such daring and determined woman was from North

Carolina. She bolted from her master's plantation sixteen times, only to be caught and returned each time.[39]

The very earliest runs to freedom were made during the colonial period by individual effort alone. Even then, some colonies had mutual agreements concerning the return of captured slave runaways. The first fugitive slave agreement took place in 1643 between the New England Confederation of Plymouth, Massachusetts, and New Haven, Connecticut. Their agreement stated, "If any servant runn away from his master into any other of these Jurisdiccons, That in such Case upon the Certyficate of one Majistrate in the Jurisdiccon out of which the said servant fled, or upon other due proofe, the said servant shall be delivered either to his Master or any other that pursues and brings such Certyficate of proofe."[40]

That was before antislavery societies and the like organized to help slaves flee from bondage. Later, Pennsylvania became the first state to pass legislation for the gradual manumission of slaves in 1780. Prior to then, slave labor was legal in all thirteen states. Therefore, a runaway had to reach Canada to the north, Spanish-held Florida or even Mexico to the south in order to breathe free air.[41]

As noted previously, it is believed that the organized effort to assist slaves with their escapes and totally frustrate their slave masters began sometime after the turn of the nineteenth century, although it could have begun a little earlier. The organization soon acquired the name the "Underground Railroad." Some evidence points to the Underground Railroad having its beginning in Pennsylvania, when there was resistance to returning an escaped female slave to her owner. The movement to assist slaves to havens in the North and Canada spread rapidly thereafter, with indications that underground means were being used in North Carolina by 1819.[42]

The "Underground Railroad" probably became the organization's unofficial title not long after the combining of the steam engine and the laying of rails. One story of how the secret network of routes and safe houses got its name was told by a former slave, writing in 1860. A very upset slave owner could not understand how his slave could manage to simply vanish. "Those damned abolitionists must have a railroad under the ground," he groused.[43]

Another account attributed to giving the Underground Railroad its name occurred in 1831. A runaway Kentucky slave made it safely across the Ohio River to freedom and disappeared completely. His master, who had been in feverish pursuit until then, finally exclaimed that his slave must have "gone off on an underground railroad."[44]

Local claims have been made that the first use of the term "Underground Railroad" was made here in the Tarheel State. Levi Coffin had an older cousin, Vestal Coffin, who had a son named Addison, who, along with his father and Levi, actively aided slaves in their flights to freedom. It is said that Addison was the first to use the expression in 1819.[45] Other explanations of how the Underground Railroad acquired its name exist many times over.

It is virtually impossible to know exactly how many slaves utilized the Underground Railroad to escape their lives of servitude. However, Governor John A. Quitman of Mississippi estimated that between 1810 and 1850 alone, the South lost 100,000 slaves to the efforts of determined abolitionists. Professor Wilbur William Seibert, an African American and history professor at Ohio State University in the late 1800s, believes Quitman's estimation to be fairly accurate and further estimates that approximately 40,000 slaves came through Ohio alone on the Underground Railroad.[46]

Of course, the Underground Railroad was neither literally underground nor literally a railroad. It was a network of secret routes known to the "conductors," who were responsible for leading runaways from one "station" or "depot" to another until they were in a free state or Canada. These routes went through vast forests, over rivers, down city streets and even into swamps, harbors and oceans. Slaves hid in barns, attics, basements and wagons with false bottoms and endured great discomfort and agony. However, it was much more than paths, wagons, houses and ships. More than anything else, the Underground Railroad was people. It consisted of slaves who were brave and determined enough to breathe freely and abolitionists who believed in freedom and equality so passionately that they were willing to aid the slaves' escapes, even in defiance of the law.

In North Carolina, it appears that the most organized area of the state with regard to the Underground Railroad was located in and around the Quaker-influenced central part of the state. Wilmington and other port towns certainly also saw their share of Underground Railroad activity. However, in many respects it might be fair to say that the individuals who managed to escape the masters and the laws of the Tarheel State were runaways. While runaways certainly took advantage of any help they might receive, many times it was the guile, cunning and intelligence of the individuals that landed them in free air.

Some of the people who worked to help runaway slaves escape their plantation bondage are well known nationally. A list of these would include Harriet Tubman, John Brown, Frederick Douglass, William Still and Levi Coffin, just to name a few. Others may not be as famous, like Austin Bearse,

Left: Harriet Tubman, circa 1885. *Courtesy of the Library of Congress.*

Right: Frederick Douglass, circa 1874. *Wikimedia.*

William Beard and William M. Mitchell. There were countless others who remain nameless simply because their names are lost to history. Due to the very secretive nature of the Underground Railroad, very few, if any, records were kept. Most of what is known about its operation comes mainly from personal narratives compiled around the time of the Civil War or later.

North Carolina proved to be a hotbed of antislavery activity due in large part to the Quaker population of the state. While Quakers in the Perquimans County area were initially involved, much of the notoriety goes to the Coffin family who settled in the Piedmont of North Carolina, specifically in the Greensboro area, today near Guilford College. Addison Coffin described the tenacious work of North Carolina Friends in regard to antislavery as "selfish unselfishness." He wrote, "Now, as to the Underground Railroad it is with some hesitation that I venture to speak of its origin and management in N.C."[47] Manumission societies had been formed in the state, and Guilford County soon became the locus for these societies. This stemmed from the legal actions in recapturing a slave, Benjamin Benson, who had been illegally captured in Delaware, brought to Guilford County and sold in 1818. The slave got word to Addison's father, Vestal, of his condition. Vestal engaged the help of Dr. George Swaim and Enoch Macy to procure the release of Benson. The slave was then quickly taken to Georgia, where he was again sold. Through various legal moves, the slave was brought back to Guilford County, where the court, amid a furor by proslavery protestors, gave Benson his freedom.

Addison Coffin notes that the beginnings of the Underground Railroad had several factors. First, although Friends agreed to manumit their slaves in 1774, many heirs refused to do so. This brought forth the manumission societies. Second, with the Missouri Compromise, many Friends fled the slave South for the Northwest, which meant fewer antislavery protesters to confront proslavery sentiments. Third, slaves began to flee to New England and Pennsylvania.[48]

> *It was while assisting this class in escaping that the idea of an organized work suggested itself to the anti-slavery men. Within a few years there was a route from Virginia to Pennsylvania, a route from Richmond, Virginia, to the Ohio River on the Virginia turnpike as it hit the Kanawha River. The Underground Railroad was in full force by 1830 with routes to Pennsylvania, Ohio, Indiana and Illinois. Stations were roughly twenty to thirty miles apart with an occasional distance of forty miles. Slaves hid in the woods or cornfields. The wonder now is that the secret was not discovered in the time intervening between 1830 and 1860, and yet so simple that a child could understand.[49]*

Coffin does not specifically say where the Underground Railroad began in North Carolina. "From the starting point in North Carolina to the great turnpike in Virginia" the route was marked by "*driving nails in trees, fences, and stumps*. Where there was a fork in the road there was a nail driven in a tree three and half feet from the ground halfway around from front to back, if the right hand road was to be taken the nail was driven on the right hand side, if the left was the road, the nail was to the left."

There were even more directions:

> *If there were fences and no tree, the nail was driven in the middle of the second rail from the top, over on the inside of the fence, to the right or left as in the trees, if neither tree, nor fence was near then a stake, or stone was so set as to be unseen by day, but found at night. When a fugitive…came to a fork in the road, they would go to the nearest tree put their arms round and rub downwards, which ever arm struck the nail, right or left, that was*

the road, and they walked right on with no mistake, so with fences, but the stakes, or stones, had to be found with their feet, which was tolerably easily done. Those who were doubtful as to their ability to remember details, would take a string and tie short pieces of string to the long one to represent the fork and cross roads, and then by tyinid notes [tying knots] *which they understood make a complete, but simple way bills that was almost unerring in its simplicity.*[50]

When the fugitives came to rivers, they could not use the ferries since ferrymen were aware of escaping slaves. Rafts were made of fence rails tied together with anything available: grapevine rope, a cord or even grass ropes. Upon arrival on the other side, the ropes were cut, and the rails were left to float downstream. Since boys typically did such destructive acts, nobody was the wiser.[51]

Many who read about the Underground Railroad might be confused about the role of the conductor. Addison Coffin points out that the conductor's main task was to keep the road marked and to make changes if and when they were necessary, especially if emergencies arose. The above system of marks was used from North Carolina through Tennessee to Kentucky. Only the conductors knew the way of the marks, and they gave this information only to escaping fugitives.[52]

Contrary to popular belief, conductors rarely went on the route with the fugitives, and that was mainly with women and children. Conductors, being Friends, did not believe in fighting for defense, so "strategy, swiftness of foot, and adroit maneuvering [sic] was the means of safety…but the whole thing depended on the thorough knowledge of the country, of all of its hills, streams, forests and hiding places, places where they could play bo-peep with impunity with horsemen." Likewise, the fugitives often found an "ability to think, to act, to plan unknown to them before was suddenly called into action, which was to them the dawning of a new life."[53]

One can imagine that conductors were often afraid, anxious and wary of anything and everybody. If caught, there were serious consequences, legal and physical, even death. Thus Coffin notes that many conductors only lasted about ten years. Some went west for a few years, where work on the Railroad "seem'd mere child's play, compared with the south." The driving forces behind such dangerous work were a sense of religious duty, a belief that the institution of slavery was actually reducing the slave owner and his family to becoming slaves to the institution of slavery and, most important, "to keep alive and intensify the agitation of the subject of slavery, to compel the indifferent to think, for a thinking community nearly always gets to thinking right on any subject."[54]

Coffin relates that in the eastern portion of North Carolina, the way of escape was much different. Escape was by water, and secret channels and byways were similarly marked yet by different means by the boatmen. Unfortunately, Coffin does not provide any further information here.

While many people today believe that all slaves who showed up at a conductor's door were piloted off to freedom, Addison Coffin adds a sobering point. Potential fugitives were scrutinized carefully before being provided the routes. Did they have the wits and stamina to withstand the stress and anxiety of the arduous and dangerous journey? Did they have the ability to hold secret the routes of escape? Surprisingly, most were turned away.

When talking about the Civil War in North Carolina, Coffin writes that "from 1862–65 there were many hundreds of young men and boys, [who] fled from the south to avoid the conscription into the southern army… and in 1864 when the conscription became universal…other hundreds of married men fled to the Ohio Valley."[55] Indeed, North Carolina had the highest desertion rate of the Confederacy.

The Underground Railroad even continued briefly after the Civil War. Addison describes his trip to bring home the family of a slave who lived near him in Indiana. After arriving back in Greensboro, Addison left with the "colored family" and the families of the southern refugees, as well as a few "young men." He recalled, "I had a motley company of over fifty, they were all dressed in homespun clothes, though clean and nice [and] were in striking contrast to the northern people." His point was that the ravages of the Civil War had placed quite a strain on the people of the South.[56]

When news of his success spread, he was asked to go back in 1866. That March, he led over one hundred back to Indiana. All of these trips were made by actual trains.

Levi Coffin and members of his family aided runaway slaves in the Piedmont region of North Carolina before ultimately moving to Indiana, because, as he stated, "Slavery and Quakerism could not prosper together."[57]

Manumission societies, of which the Friends were instrumental, were notably concentrated in and around Guilford, Randolph and Alamance Counties. These societies were dedicated not only to the abolition of slavery, but they also actively aided runaway slaves in their escape to areas of the North where slaves had been emancipated or to Canada.

The coastal section of North Carolina was another hive of Underground Railroad interest. Ports like New Bern and Washington were places where escapes were made aboard ships sailing north to Philadelphia, Boston and New York. However, the prime port for slaves seeking freedom was the state's largest and busiest port, Wilmington. One Rocky Point planter referred to neighboring Wilmington as "an asylum for Runaways."[58] It is easy to see why, since Wilmington had a large African American population among whom escapees could become lost until an opportunity to sail presented itself.

One particular area that proved to be a runaway's haven and a slave's hell was the Dismal Swamp, which straddles the border between North Carolina and Virginia. This desolate section near the coast of both states was mutually a sanctuary for runaways and a place of misery and danger for those still in slavery. Numerous blacks fleeing captivity used the Dismal Swamp to hide out temporarily until a dash to the North could be arranged, usually escaping aboard a northbound ship sailing out of Norfolk or Portsmouth. However, crews of slaves were sent into the swamp for weeks on end to cut and tow out cypress and oaks by the thousands.[59] All the while, they were fending off deadly snakes and mosquitoes carrying sickness.

The Dismal Swamp Canal as it appears today. *Courtesy of Lee C. Miller.*

The coastal plains region of North Carolina was easily the area of the state with the most slaves. Therefore, coastal ports and rivers were alive with Underground Railroad activity. While the Piedmont region of the state certainly had a number of slaves, they were not as numerous as along the fertile coast and lowland section. Yet, as evidenced by the presence of the manumission societies around the geographic center of North Carolina, the less fertile clay soil still resulted in many slaves attempting escape.

Due to soil and topography and, as compared to the rest of the state, the absence of huge amounts of personal wealth, the antebellum mountainous region of North Carolina yielded few slaves. Here, the soil was not rich and flat like the coastal region and certainly didn't contain the sparse pockets of farmable land that could be found in the Piedmont area. As a result, slaves, at least in the numbers found to the East, simply did not exist.

When the picture is taken as a whole, it should not be surprising that human beings would look for means—even desperate means—to escape the humiliation of being mere property. Even those slaves who were treated well, according to the standards of the time, could not claim the title of "freedman." Until they could manage to put a considerable distance between themselves and a life of constant toil, untold suffering from whips, chains, slave codes intended to "keep them in their place" and cruel masters, they could not hope for the life of even a white subsistence farmer.

To the extent that the Underground Railroad existed in North Carolina, it was with the assistance of determined antislavery individuals, both black and white, and groups like the manumission societies. However, to the degree that men and women, born and bought into human bondage, fulfilled the dream of becoming full members of the American dream, their own resolve, industriousness, energy and cleverness cannot be underestimated.

Chapter 3

RUNAWAYS AND THE NORTH CAROLINA LAW

I n the late summer of 1769, a young African American man, twenty-five years of age, stole something very valuable from a plantation owner whose name was John Lucas of Bladen, North Carolina. The stolen item was the young black man himself. His name was William, and according to his master, he was a good cooper, probably a barrel maker. William became a runaway on September 11, according to an advertisement placed in the November 24 edition of the *Cape Fear Mercury*.

John Lucas goes to great lengths in the advertisement to describe his slave. Besides giving his age, Lucas's ad states that William is "about 5 feet 8 inches high; is well made, has lost some of his Upper fore-Teeth, is Country born, Sensible, and speaks English very well." Lucas goes on to offer five pounds to anyone who secured his slave so that he might have him again.[60]

Masters placing advertisements concerning runaway slaves was not an uncommon occurrence. In the same issue of the *Cape Fear Mercury* in which William's escape appears, another advertisement is posted concerning a runaway named Richmond, from Wilmington. Also in that issue, Christopher Cains, the sheriff of Brunswick County, announces the sale, during the next session of the Superior Court, of "Six likely Country-born slaves." Since the sale was instigated by the sheriff, it is appropriate to assume that the six men in the advertisement were most likely runaways themselves, who, for whatever reasons, had never been claimed.

Again, in the November 24, 1769 issue of the *Cape Fear Mercury*, there is another advertisement under the headline of, "Taken Up and Committed to Jail." In this ad, Onslow County sheriff Lewis Williams relates details of "Four likely Negro Men." The sheriff describes one of the men as probably exceeding forty years of age due to the grey hair on his head and beard. He indicates the other three appear to be younger. None of the four men speak English, and they each possess a striped Dutch blanket, therefore the sheriff surmises that they are not native born.

Runaways were not a new phenomenon in the eighteenth century. Almost from the first introduction of Africans to the Carolina economy, those in perpetual servitude began attempting to flee the shackles that bound them. By the decade of the 1680s, planters were already grousing that their Negros were running off to St. Augustine, Florida.[61] Therefore, as slaves ran away and eluded their masters, coupled with the growth in the black population, the fact that owning a slave was a significant investment and the growing fear of slave rebellion, it was just a matter of time before they sought out some legal means of controlling their chattel.

As a result, as early as 1699 the colonial legislature of North Carolina took a significant step toward confronting the dilemma of runaways. However, the law was more of an attempt to control the behavior of whites and others that might aid runaways than an attempt to control the behavior of slaves. Anyone found guilty of facilitating the escape of a slave or an indentured servant would be fined ten shillings for every night and forced to pay for any damages that could be substantiated by the runaway's owner.[62]

It is significant to note that the 1699 law does not speak to what was to be the punishment of the runaways. It speaks only to what penalties those aiding and abetting runaways would be required to face by the colony. The culture of the time and tradition, however, would prescribe that the captured fugitives would suffer badly at the hands of their masters. They would almost certainly suffer the terrible sting of the whip, with multiple lashes. Other possible punishments might include the amputation of toes or perhaps part of the runaway's foot, although that was usually reserved for slaves who had attempted multiple escapes. Branding the escapee in some manner, giving him or her additional duties or possibly cropping one or both ears were also inflicted in order to serve as a reminder to not try stealing themselves again.[63]

Being dominant politically, the wealthy landowners who were the portion of the citizenry most likely to own slaves would not allow slaves to run away with impunity for long. By 1715, North Carolina's colonial legislature had enacted a systematic slave code. The code addressed wide-ranging slave behaviors.

According to the 1715 act, which was patterned after the Virginia and South Carolina codes, slaves were not allowed to leave their respective plantations without written permission from their owners or overseers. These passes, or tickets, as they were often called, were to state the name of the slave, indicate where the slave's home plantation was located and where they were headed. Masters who allowed their bondsmen to leave their home plantation without these passes could be fined five shillings, plus the slave was deemed to be a runaway.

Further, anyone taking a slave into custody was to be paid at least five shillings by the slave's owner. They were also liable for one shilling per mile of transport up to ten miles and three shillings per mile for every mile above ten miles. If the owner could not be located, the captor was to take the slave to the nearest law enforcement agency, which would compensate the catcher. Once the owner was located by the law enforcement agency, the owner would then be obligated to reimburse the local authorities for their expenses, which would include six pence per day for lodgings.[64]

Aside from slave behavior, the behavior of all blacks—even free blacks—and Native Americans came under the purview of these colonial laws. One example of the effects of these acts began in 1703, when many free blacks, it appears, had the audacity to vote. In 1705, some white residents of the North Carolina colony complained that "all sorts of people, even servants, Negros, Aliens, Jews and Common sailors were admitted to vote in Elections." Such actions were dealt with in 1715, by a law that stated, "No person whatsoever Inhabitant of this Government born out of the Allegiance of his Majesty and not made free no Negro Mullatto or Indians shall be capable of voting for Members of Assembly."[65]

One paramount concern of slave masters and all whites in general was the possibility of a slave uprising. By 1739, the South Carolina colony had a black population that outnumbered the white inhabitants by two to one, which did not go unnoticed by the whites. On September 9 of that year, in a revolt now known as Stono's Rebellion, roughly sixty to one hundred slaves were met by slave owners in a fierce confrontation that resulted in the death of about twenty whites, with double that number of dead slaves.[66]

Stono's Rebellion sent shudders through the white colonists of the South, and the political leaders of North Carolina certainly took notice. Therefore, North Carolina's General Assembly passed another slave code act in 1741 that, like the 1715 legislation, was patterned to a large degree on similar legislation in South Carolina. It further attempted to plug any gaps that could be exploited by slaves to escape and, in particular, cause harm to whites.

One requirement of the statute was that local sheriffs who had come into possession of runaways were to publish a full description of them that was to consist of height, complexion, identifiable bodily marks and clothing. Copies of the description were to be passed around to local church officials, who were then obligated to post them in an "open and convenient place" for two months. In order to discourage law enforcement officials from maintaining runaway slaves for themselves, a penalty of five pounds would be charged if they did not properly give notice of their capture.[67]

Perhaps the most formidable aspect of the 1741 statute was that which addressed slaves in possession of any weapons. The law specified clearly that slaves were not to be "armed with Gun, Sword, Club or other Weapon, or shall keep any such Weapon, or shall Hunt or Range in the Woods," except when in possession of a written certificate from his master. Slaves who were in violation of this portion of the act would get twenty lashes. If slave masters owned slaves who were to retain weapons as part of their duties, the slave owner was compelled to provide in writing the names of any Negros who used weapons.[68]

In 1753, the General Assembly provided for a patrol system in the colony. Each county justice of the peace was to divide his county into districts and appoint three freeholders in these districts to be searchers. The searchers were authorized to search all slave quarters in the districts in order to potentially locate weapons the slaves may have concealed in their meager dwellings.

These patrols were set up to try to find hidden weapons, but they were not patrols in the sense that they were empowered to look for and capture runaways and others who may have been off of their respective plantations without permission. In response to runaways, as well as the possibility that their bondsmen might be planning a rebellion, some eastern counties provided for patrols that were used in a more traditional function in 1775. It is no coincidence the whites' movement toward independence from the British had stirred a desire for liberty from their chattel as well. One dire aspect of these patrols in Pitt, Craven and New Hanover Counties was that any slave who was off his or her master's property and would not yield to the patrollers could be shot instantly.[69]

In North Carolina and throughout the South though, there was usually hesitation to mete out the ultimate penalty for the very simple reason that slaves represented an investment on the part of the slave master. Even in cases of the rape of a white woman, arson and when conspiracy to revolt against the established order could be proved, taking the life of a slave was a last resort, not only because of the lost investment but also because the slaveholder also lost the slave's potential labor. Further, any white slave owner who responded to a slave's crimes by severely whipping him or taking his life knew there was the possibility of the same happening to one or more of their slaves by another owner.[70]

State and local slave codes continued to be adopted and adapted until the end of the Civil War in 1865, including the federal Fugitive Slave Acts of 1793 and 1850, which provided for the return of escaped slaves to their owners. Even those who managed to make their way to a free state were expected to be returned if captured. Magistrates in the North who judged a black man or woman to be a runaway and ruled that they be returned to the person claiming them were financially compensated.

The debate concerning fugitive slaves entered into the Constitution during the composition of the document in 1787. As it was passed by the convention and ratified by the states, Article IV, Section 2, reads in part, "No Person held to Service or Labor in one State, under the laws thereof, escaping into another, shall, in Consequence of any Law or Regulation therein, be discharged from such Service or Labor, but shall be delivered up on Claim of the Party to whom such Service or Labor may be due."[71] In laymen's terms, it means simply that if a person who is a slave under the laws of a slave state enters into a free state, the free state is obligated to return the slave to its owner, and the slave owner or his agent may enter the free slave state to capture the slave.

In order to put even more teeth into what became known as the Constitution's "Fugitive Slave Clause," Congress passed the Fugitive Slave Act of 1793. The law stipulated that the federal magistrates in free states were to confirm accused runaways for extradition to slave states. Pennsylvania, in a move meant to protect its free black citizens from scurrilous slave catchers, enacted a personal liberty statute. However, the Supreme Court declared Pennsylvania's statute unconstitutional in 1842.[72]

One of the most controversial laws ever passed by Congress and signed by a president was the Fugitive Slave Act of 1850. Under the 1850 act, more than nine hundred purported slaves were extradited to slave states between 1850 and 1861.[73] It was more punitive than the 1793 law in that it negated due process assurances like trial by jury. It was the result of an attempted compromise between the abolitionist North and slaveholding South. The compromise's bonding effect, to whatever degree it was ever effective, only lasted eleven years.

For escapees, especially in the eastern region of North Carolina, the Dismal Swamp, covering an area from Edenton to Norfolk in Virginia, was quite frequently a haven. One person indicated that, with its thick forests and dangerous waters, those choosing to live there were perfectly safe from pursuit. One traveler in 1777 suggested that the Dismal Swamp "was infested by concealed royalists, and runaway negros [*sic*], who could not be approached with safety."[74]

A look at runaway advertisements reveals that slaves fleeing their bonds were not just from the eastern region of North Carolina, however. Many times they were attempting to escape to the east because of the possibility of making their way north on ships. But one advertisement in the March 24, 1830 edition of *the Greensborough Patriot* reveals that even in a quiet Piedmont county with Quakers and manumission societies, like Randolph County, slavery existed and slaves were attempting escape. The advertisement reads in part, "$50 REWARD, RANAWAY from the subscriber on, or about February last, a bright Mulatto man named Nelson…Any person apprehending said Mulatto and delivering him to me in the south east of Randolph County." It continues to offer the aforementioned reward, or twenty-five dollars if lodged in jail.[75]

As with any enterprise, scores of slaves from North Carolina were able to escape their bonded lives and live the life of a free person in New England, Canada and sometimes even Florida or Mexico, while others breathed free for mere hours or days before being returned to certain cruel, harsh punishment. Yet the desire to live freely was so overwhelming that the laws and punishments of the state and nation, as well as the traditional beatings and brandings of the slave owner class did not deter black men and women from searching desperately for a means to break away.

Chapter 4

WHO WERE THE SLAVES?

L ook at stories of slaves in the histories of the Underground Railroad or even in some extensive works on blacks and slavery in early America and you often will see something missing: the slaves themselves. Who were the actual slaves who fled the tobacco fields, corn rows, plantation houses, wharves and blacksmith sheds?

Fortunately, we can examine runaway slave ads from North Carolina newspapers. From these accounts, fugitives often appear as the caricature silhouetted black man with the bundle of clothes tied up on a stick carried on his shoulder that appeared in numerous runaway slave ads. However, if we look closer through the digitized collection of runaway slave ads of North Carolina, we can get a better picture of who a runaway might actually be.

First, some statistics are in order. According to census data in 1790, there were 289,143 whites in North Carolina. Just over 5,000 free blacks lived in the Tarheel State, as did 102,726 slaves. In this same year there were 16,310 families who owned one or more slaves. Slaves made up 25 percent of the population in 1790.

By 1860, while the numbers had increased, the percentages were about the same. In that year, 629,942 whites lived in the state, as compared to 30,463 free blacks. There were 331,059 slaves, 33 percent of the population.[76]

What did the slave face if he or she ran away? A 1741 law noted that a captured slave would have one ear nailed to a wall, and then the ear would be cut off; likewise the other ear, and then the slave would be whipped with thirty-nine lashes. This was actually better than another law of the same year that gave any person who captured a slave permission to "kill and destroy such Slave or Slaves by such Ways and Means as he or she shall think fit." In 1787, the slave Darby was put in jail, and on the next day, he was tied to a stake and burned to death.[77] Somewhere between mutilation and death was the great bulk of punishments. And that was not a great span of difference for the captured slave. These draconian laws were eventually erased as owners began to slowly treat runaway slaves better.

When we look at runaway slave ads, we find real persons, humans instead of chattel, personalities rather than generic terms like "plantation slaves" or "slaves who worked in the Big House." The albeit brief descriptions tell us what the owners thought and knew and remembered and, often times, what they could not recall about their slaves.[78]

Names provide a broad view of the North Carolina slave. "A likely Negro fellow and Wench, by the names of Peter and Hagar" ran one March 20, 1800 ad from Anson County. There was Quaco, a male blacksmith from near Wilmington who "squints much, and has a drawling tone when he speaks"; Auston and Coartney, who ran away from Stantonsburg to Sparta in 1833; "a mulatto fellow named Bill"; Trim, who robbed his owner and fled for Wilmington in 1797; Jerry Randall, who was a rarity because he had a first and last name; Ransom, who was a "very noted fellow"; Hannah, who "was above the common size," suggesting that slaves were of a particular stature, and she displayed a "very pleasing countenance"; Will; a young boy named Jack; Lucy, who "goes about finely dressed"; and Wincy, who fled Wakefield to find her mother in nearby Raleigh in 1839. Some slaves had several names or aliases, such as Ned and Jacob, who were also known as Sweat and Rogers. There was a slave named Hardy; Patty was "black and lusty made."

Some men had rather feminine names: Valentine and Steppeny were two. Sometimes a family fled together, as was the case of Peter, Dinah and their eight-month-old son Simon. Toney was a bit contradictory because he "has a sly look and speaks very polite." Shade had lost four fingers due to an "accident with an axe"; this type of description was quite common. Tuesday, a male slave, "went off without provocation." Some names had a noble character: Cesar, Moses, Pluto. Others were biblical (or Hebrew): Ruth, Abram, Abner, Levin, Aaron, David. A few left much to the imagination, like Brister, while others, like Drew, seemed a bit upper class. Phereba, despite the exotic sound of her name, was only worth eight dollars. A male named Walkfa was described as one who had a "long head and was fully lusty as a common Fellow." Moll was a female slave of slender build, and one is left to

Twenty Dollars Reward.

RANAWAY from the Subscriber on the first day of January last, a negro woman between thirty and thirty-five years of age by the name of LUNER. She is about five feet high, with a small scar on her forehead. She formerly belonged to John Waddell, and is likely to be lurking about Alfred Waddell's in Brunswick county. The above reward will be given to any person that will bring her to me, or lodge her in jail so that I get her again.

ROBERT COUNCIL.

Near Westbrooks Post Office, }
Bladen County, N. C. }   191-5t.

An 1839 slave advertisement in the *Salisbury Western Carolinian*.

wonder what Scrub, a slave from Orange County, looked like. Needham and Summer fled together, but they were not husband and wife: both were men. Jude had very long hair.

Physical marks were often part of the descriptions in the runaway slave ads. Some had scars on their faces and heads, and these could be covered with various styles of hair or braids as in the case of Tom, who escaped from a Pittsboro jail while wearing an iron collar in 1814 and covered his head scar by "platting his hair over it." Other scars were on wrists and knees; some slaves were missing portions of their ears from biting in fights. Digits might be bent or missing from hands. Many slaves were knock-kneed, bow-legged or had a limp or toes that stuck out. Numerous slaves had lost toes due to frostbite and the fact that slaves only received one pair of shoes—if that—per year. One had "a remarkable singular mark on the right side of his nose," while another had a large scar on one shoulder. Many slaves stuttered; some looked downward, an important note since slaves were not to look directly at their masters or other whites. Peter was "apt to smile when spoken to." Some slaves were "spare made" or "well made" or "slim but also genteel." Many were missing teeth, and some had yellow hair. Various brandings are described, and one was described as having a "very coarse voice."

David was "tolerably black, has a handsome face, small hands and uncommon white teeth," while many other slaves were noted as having "an impudent look." One slave had large whiskers and another walked on a "remarkable long narrow foot." One might expect that many slaves had a "bushy head of hair." Joe was missing a toe, and his other teeth were crooked, along with a gap in his teeth. One slave had very long fingers. Bate, who escaped from a brickyard, bore a scar on his elbow from a burn.

In one 1790 ad from Montgomery County, Toby, who landed in Charleston just a few years before and spoke broken English, "has his country mark on both sides of his face." Was this a tribal brand? Luke had a brand of "WC" on his cheek. This may have been the initials of an owner, since twenty-one-year-old Prince, a Guinea-born slave of Pitt County who spoke good English, had a "WG" branded on both of his cheeks, which were interestingly the initials of his owner, William Grimes. Many slaves were so well known that no description was necessary for the ad.

Skin tones ran the spectrum. A slave might be coal black, very black, mulatto, yellowish in complexion, of light complexion or near white. Many owners used facial features to distinguish their slaves from others. Scars are a consistent marking, around eyes, ears, scalps, jaws and mouths. Needham had an "aquiline [resembles an eagle's beak] nose." Other times the African roots were quite clear, as when a slave was described as "lips tolerably thick." Vocal ticks were used as means to identify a runaway: "talks with a lisp," "man of fair speech," "somewhat of an impediment in his speech" or "quick spoken." Ben had "a fierce look and a fine voice." One slave had more freckles than most slaves. One unnamed mulatto boy had an "impertinent face." Lewis had a face full of "bumps or pimples."

Sixteen-year-old Delia, all four feet ten inches of her, who was of yellow complexion with "large breasts," fled from Montgomery County with Jack, leaving behind an eight-month-old boy. This is quite odd: usually babies were taken with the slaves. Was this baby the result of rape? Dave was "slender made, yellow complexion, down look when spoken to, speaks not very quick when spoken to; has not got good eyes, on account of having wild hairs in them at all times." Dolphus, of Perquimans County, was "large and clumsy." Peter, of Chatham County, was of "stout built" and "board faced"; Harry was a "little grey about the Temples, his Hair, when grown, very bushy, between Wool and Hair; Thin Visage, soft, smiling Speech, and rather under middle Size"; and Davy and Tom had "both been whipped severely for stealing as their Backs will show." In Randolph County, Isaac's back, among other physical features, was "well-marked with a hickory." Jasper was "very bow-legged."

It is a wonder that Jack, "a tolerable shoemaker," was even alive. "He has a scar on his forehead, and a part of one of his upper foreteeth broken off, one of his wrists broke and crooked, and his right leg pretty much shot with small shot which will shew [*sic*] very plainly." Tom was missing his right ear, as was his partner, who accompanied him on his flight to freedom. Sometimes the marking had a story to tell: six-foot-tall Jim had a scar on his neck that was "occasioned by a rising," as in an uprising. That might have been reflected in the price for his capture: five dollars. Fifty-five-year-old Bob, who was "somewhat gray," also had "a large scar on one of his feet, occasioned by the cut of an axe; the inside of the fingers on one of his hands, his right it is believed, has been cut off with a scythe, and he has two lumps, one on his neck and one on his breast." Little wonder that he was only worth five dollars in 1822. Crawford was short but also of "swarthy complexion nearly white, broad face and down look, no beard, straight hair not very black, very full breast." Sally was "very fleshy, rather low and not very black." Mudean had large facial features and had lost some of the small toes off of one or both feet. Alford, who had a "sprightly appearance" and was quite "talkative," left with a "blue cloth coat and slick hat" along with a "bombazet frock coat" and other things and "will probably appear quite respectably clad."

What is sometimes a bit whimsical is what they carried off with them in their escape. Yet when we realize that they could not take all of their precious few possessions, the items that were carted away demonstrate what was of most importance to them. Some carried a coat or coats, pantaloons or other form of legwear, often of brightly colored cloth, which begs the question why a runaway would wear anything bright; one unnamed runaway had a fur hat and "other forms of negro clothing." Nearly all wore some form of homespun cotton cloth dresses or pants; at least two scurried away cutlasses, most likely stolen from the master. Ajaz took so many different clothes that his owner, William Graves Berry, could not describe him in the 1807 ad. In that same year, John Williams of Chatham County advertised that two mulattoes had run away with "two horses, a dark brown gelding and iron grey mare, complete with an old saddle, lead lines, bits and bridle, clothes, fiddle and meal bag," as well as two firearms. It would be difficult to hide the horses on a journey to freedom. Were they to be sold or ridden? Interestingly, there was only a twenty-dollar reward for all of this—slaves, horses, tack and fiddle.

Jim took with him "a quantity of fine clothes" and a "large, fierce yellow Dog." What if the dog barked, revealing the runaway? One male slave stole a pitching axe. Martin, who escaped in 1811, wore the typical woolen handmade pantaloons and shirt, but he also took with him "a suit of Sunday cloaths [sic]" as well. Dave took with him "forty or fifty dollars in cash." Bob, who fled in 1826, took some clothes, and he "had also a double eased silver Watch marked Norton, London, N. 334 with D. Scotts Watch bill, in the case." Ames stole a small bay mare when he fled to Wilmington. Lewis carried with him a watch and pocket organ. Peter, a coastal slave, scurried off with a sailboat and two sails. Bill, who was a "tolerable shoemaker," predictably took with him his tools, yet he also absconded with "a quantity of manufactured tobacco." John, also known as Jack, fled Montgomery County for Norfolk, Virginia, with "some books, one Testament, one Scott's lesson, one hymn book, one printed note book and Spelling book."

Runaway slave ads reveal much information about the varied skills of slaves at this time. A slave might be a blacksmith or cook or play fiddle or violin. Toney was known as a hewer, timber-getter and shipyard worker. Some could read, in clear violation of an act of law in North Carolina in 1830–31, and quite a few slave ads warned that the slave could write his or her own free pass. Jim, who had a scar under one eye and was missing some portion of one ear, was noted for his skills as a cobbler and cooper, very handy with tools and was "fond of spirits." Ruth, a "NEGRO WENCH," from Chatham County, was noted for speaking both Dutch and English. Harry, aka Henry Hudson or other aliases, was "very handy in all Kinds of Plantation-Business, as well as a coarse Shoe-maker and rough Carpenter." One unnamed slave "follows the barber business." Willis, who escaped in 1811, was a "tolerable" shoemaker, but he also was known to exhort or preach, thus he stole a Bible and took it with him. (The irony of a preacher stealing a Bible is too much.) Peter, fleeing his master in Perquimans County, took his cobblering tools with him. Forty-year-old Tom likewise might pass himself off as a preacher because he could "tell a good tale." Charles played the fiddle. Dolphus tries to pass himself off as a carpenter but "knows nothing of the business."

One of the major revelations from the runaway slave ads is their travel plans. Rare is the ad that features the "typical" North Carolina Underground Railroad scenario such as these examples:

TEN DOLLARS REWARD

MADE his escape, on the 16th instant, near Hertford, in Perquimans, my negro fellow JOB; he is about 5 feet 6 inches high, rather black, has remarkable small feet and hands, 25 or 30 years of age; he was bred in Perquimans, and probably he may be lurking about there, as he has a mother and other relations not far from Hertford, he was one of the negroes emancipated by the Quakers, and taken up and sold by order of court; it is

more than probable that they may wish to secret him; all those who offend that way, may rely on being dealt with in the utmost severity of the law. The above reward will be given to any person that will deliver said negro me, or confine him in gaol [jail] *so that I get him again, together with all reasonable expences* [sic].
THOMAS POOL.
Pasequetank, Nov. 28, 1796.[79]

Likewise, Peter and Jude did not even leave Perquimans County, a known Quaker area, when they escaped. According to the ad placed by William Whedbee in 1796, they were believed to be "lurking in this county" at John and Mary Blount's residence. Were they hoping to hitch a ride on the Quaker road to freedom?

$20
Reward.
Ran away from the Subscriber, living in Montgomery County, on Monday the 30th of December last,
A Negro Man, named Peter, And his Wife, named Nan.
Peter is about 6 feet high, 30 years old, spare made, of a dark complexion, and a pleasant countenance; he has a scar on his right foot.
Nan is about the middle size, about 28 years old, of a yellow complexion, and has a scar on her nose.
They have been heard of in Randolph County, under false names: Peter called himself Walter, and Nan took the name of Polly. It is supposed they are aiming for a free State, in company with two other negroes.
I will give the above reward to any person who will lodge them in any jail, and notify me of the same.
WILLIAM HARRIS. Montgomery County, N.C. }
January 27, 1834. }[80]

In regards to the latter ad, when coupled with a few more runaway ads from Montgomery County, a pattern emerges. There is a definite direction: north from Montgomery County through Randolph County, which then leads to Guilford County. Randolph and Guilford Counties were Quaker strongholds, and most likely some slaves in the middle portion of North Carolina were hoping for a passage to freedom using the Quakers. This could very well be the case behind this ad:

$10 or $25 Reward.

RANAWAY on Tuesday last, a bright Mulatto BOY, about 21 or 22 years of age, about 5 feet 9 or 10 inches high, spare made. He will no doubt attempt to pass for a free man. It is believed that he will endeavor to get to a free State. It is known that he intended making his way through Randolph and Guilford Counties.

To any person apprehending said Boy, and confining him so that I get him, I will give $10 if taken within the State, and $25 if taken without.

Any information respecting said Boy will be thankfully received, addressed to the Subscriber at Lawrenceville, Montgomery County, N.C.

THOMAS PEMBERTON.

May 25, 1839.[81]

The dates and directions fit well within the timeframe of Quaker assistance in the Piedmont of North Carolina. Another ad from Randolph County also fits the *modus operandi* for Quakers of that time. Sometimes the ad reveals confusion from the subscriber, who no doubt reflected the confusion of his own slave. In 1808, Davy escaped from Chatham County, perhaps again since the ad notes he might run *back* to Ohio, a free state. But he might also be en route to Jones County in North Carolina, to his previous owner (who brought him back from Ohio?). One slave who looked like an Indian was believed to be traveling in 1830 with a white man and another black man. He was headed north to western Virginia for the free states. Henry headed for Indiana in 1835.

Not all fugitives sought freedom on the continent. Early slave ads reveal the initial foreign roots of slaves in North Carolina. In 1796, Anthony and John, who both spoke English and French, left their Pitt County bondage and headed east for a port city, most likely headed back to the West Indies. A "French negro fellow" also escaped from Greenville in 1796, and this possibly links the slave to some of the Caribbean islands where French was spoken. Haiti was also listed as the possible destination for some slaves. Anthony escaped his bondage from Randolph County slaveowner Joshua Craven and headed toward Wilmington by way of Fayetteville, probably en route to "Hayti."

One ad reveals that slaves often helped other slaves, including family, escape north:

$100 Reward.

RAN AWAY from the subscriber, on Wednesday night last, my negro woman

CHANEY,

Aged about 40 years, slender built, bright mulatto—about the sight of one of her eyes she has a white speck. Chaney took with her, her three children— MARY, aged 11 or 12 years, mahogany color—LAZARUS, aged about 4 years, bright mulatto, nearly white—and TOM, about 2 years old, mulatto color. I have been informed, that Godwin Cotton's Eli has of late frequently visited Chaney, and in all probability will assist her in getting to a free State. The above reward will be given for the apprehension of Chaney and her three children, if delivered to me near Falkland, Pitt county, NC or if confined in any jail so that I get them again. All persons are forbid harboring or carrying off said negroes under penalty of the law.
JOSIAH BARRETT.
March 15, 1839.[82]

The 1809 ad from John Baker of Brunswick County reveals the initial Tarheel State destinations of many slaves, especially those in the eastern portion of the state: New Bern, Washington County, Edenton, Wilmington and Beaufort. All of these are connected to coastal waters. Many, as in the case of Nero in 1820, would aim for these coastal ports and areas in hopes of setting sail north to freedom. Numerous ads have warnings for ship captains who might entertain thoughts of aiding a slave to freedom. But some towns also featured railroads, which might have been the draw for Steppeny, who fled to Wilmington "or the Railroad" in 1839.

Overall, most of the ads poke holes in the notion of an extensive "Underground Railroad" in North Carolina. Many slaves, like Jacob, pined for former owners. In 1816, Daniel fled his Montgomery County servitude and, it was believed, headed east for Currituck by way of Fayetteville and New Bern. In a 1797 *Wilmington Gazette* ad, the subscriber reveals that his escaped slaves might be with other slaves, with free blacks or hidden away on a ship. Hannah might have been harbored among free blacks or with "the lower order of white people" in Robeson County, where she had worked the year before. Cuff, who fled Montgomery County with a wool hat, shirt and trousers in 1795 "and drinks no spirits," was probably longing for his wife, who was on a plantation near the mouth of the Cape Fear River. Yellow-complexioned Larry, who fled a Belvedere plantation, was supposed to have made for the northwest (in relation to the plantation, not the northwestern part of North Carolina) or the rivers toward the coast and possibly to his former owner on a riverboat. Likewise Allen, from Randolph County, was heading northwest to Hertford or Northampton Counties near the Virginia line.

A slave might run east from, say Hillsborough, to Raleigh then Fayetteville en route to Wilmington. Or west, as in the case of thirty-year-old Lion, who fled from Pitt County to Chatham County, where he was raised. Or one could head north, as in the case of Jimmy, who ran from Brunswick County to Wayne County in 1799, just a few county lines away. Teenaged Hannah, however, fled her Brunswick County bondage for Charleston, South Carolina, by way of Wilmington. Some simply ran away back to their previous owners or to places where they were raised. This was the case for forty-year-old Charles, who fled from Chatham County back to Pitt County, where he was raised and owned by Josiah Lawrence. Some slaves, like Ephraim or Paris, fled back to the Eastern Shore of Maryland, not to escape slavery so much as perhaps because they preferred the more independent labors of the shore and sea as opposed to working on an inland North Carolina farm. Scrub left his Orange County owner for Norfolk, his former residence where, it was feared, he would head to sea for his freedom.

Billy, in 1831, fled his Rockingham owner William Bethel for New Bern by way of Hillsborough and Raleigh. Tom, David (who cloaked his "villainy" by pretending "to be religious" and "singing psalms") and Jesse (a "Virginia mulattoe" [*sic*]) ran away from their Pensacola, Yancey County home in 1828, probably aiming to go all the way across the Tarheel State back to Craven County, where they had been purchased. Likewise Moses, sometimes known as Phil, who ran from his new Wilkes County home back to Perquimans County nearly thirty years before.

East was not the only direction taken. In 1822, Caesar fled the port town of Beaufort for the Piedmont town of Hillsborough. One couple fled west to Murfreesboro, as far west as one could go in North Carolina and where they had been purchased. Bill ran west, probably to Carrol County, Tennessee, from the middle of the Tarheel State in 1826, carrying with him "four full suits, two hats, two pair of shoes, one superfine black broad-cloath coat; one great coat of the very best quality, line[d] with new red flannel; between 40 and 50 dollars, about $30 specie."

Others might have fled straight north, although this is more speculation based on limited information in the ads. Samuel left behind his Orange County bondage in 1828 for Philadelphia or New York, typical Underground Railroad sites of this time, where it was believed he would seek passage on a ship. Osborn ran north to a free state in 1835. Anthony, of Randolph County, either fled to the Deep South (a notoriously dangerous place for any black person) to be near his wife or to a free state in 1837. Sometimes the owner had no idea where the slave was headed. Dick, a blacksmith, had already escaped twice, headed for Ohio at least once, and was believed to be headed west again in 1832 or to Wilmington or New Bern in hopes of finding ship passage north.

The value of a runaway slave varied widely. Clumsy Dolphus was worth only $5, but Edah, a beautiful mulatto with "modest pretty countenance, red cheeks, and a remarkable handsome figure" who worked more as a free servant than a household slave, according to her master, was worth $50 if found in state, $100 if found outside of North Carolina. It was feared she had been stolen or wooed away. It is beyond the scope of this book to cover all the counties, but a comparison of ads from Orange County, which was in the Piedmont area and thus notably less given to slaves, with Carteret County, a coastal area, provides some perspective. We begin with Orange County in the late 1700s.

In 1784, twenty-five-year-old Scrub ran away from his owner, Richard Benneham, who offered thirty dollars for his capture and return. Scrub had many skills: groomsman, gardener, wagoner and hostler (one who cares for horses and mules). He was also described as strong, active and of good countenance, as well as honest and trustworthy.

In 1797, William Mebane advertised for a runaway named Derry, who was twenty-seven years old. He was of the same build as Scrub, but no skills were listed for him. He was distinguished only by a scar of some type that left a white, hairless spot on his scalp. Reward: five dollars. Twenty years later, the captor of forty-year-old Britain would also receive five dollars for his troubles. The mulattoes Duncan and Jim were only worth five dollars each in 1818.

Mary Doherty advertised in the 1790s for the slave Nell, thirty-one years old, very black and small, who fled the mansion of Robert Freeman. No amount was listed in the ad. The thirty-year-old "negro wench" Sally, who was about the same age as Nell and ran away to Wilmington and supposedly to her husband there in 1797, was worth five dollars, according to her owner, Richard Quince. Twenty-five-year-old Nancy was worth twenty dollars to her owner, William Kirkland, in 1808. Twenty-five-year-old Hannah, who was of a yellowish complexion, was worth fifteen dollars in 1812. Eighteen-year-old Priscilla was worth twenty dollars just six years later.

The difference in value of couples reveals no rhyme or reason. In 1800, Archibald Campbell lost two slaves, one a twenty-three- to twenty-four-year-old "strong built" male, and a "Woman of yellow complection [sic], and pleasant Countenance about the same age." They headed west to Murfreesboro, where they had been purchased just months before. Together, they were worth twenty dollars. In 1812, Peter and Polly were valued at twenty-five dollars or "a proportion part for either of them." Charles, who was thirty-five, and his wife, Lucy, seventeen, brought a reward of fifty dollars if captured, as the 1814 ad noted. Thirty-year-old Sylva, who was five months pregnant, and her thirteen-year-old son, Kimber, were collectively worth only ten dollars in 1824. Gender may not have affected the values much: when Martin and Jacob fled their bondage in 1811, they were valued together at twenty-five dollars. Coffen and Jack, who fled in 1813, however, would only merit twenty dollars total if captured.

Sometimes the value depended on logistics. In 1800, Harry, thirty-seven years old, who was a shoemaker and carpenter and could read, was worth $5 if caught locally, $10 if captured farther away. It was believed he headed to Maryland or Virginia, where he had lived previously, but that his ultimate destination was Pennsylvania. In 1811, Prince was reported as missing, but he might have also been "chased away" (as in stolen). If found alone, he was worth $20, but if he was indeed stolen, then the thief and Prince were worth a total of $100. In 1825, Dave headed for Virginia. His owner, John Vincent, would pay $50 for his capture out of state, $25 if apprehended in state.

Dick was twenty-four years old when he escaped in 1800 from William Kirkland. He was yellow-skinned, "stout and well-made" and worth fifty dollars if apprehended and brought back to the owner in Hillsborough or thirty dollars if placed in jail anywhere in the state for the owner to come and get him. On the other hand, tall and lusty Cooper, who fled from Haw River, was worth only ten dollars. Likewise Wilson, who escaped from Hillsborough in 1804. In 1825, Ben, who was sixty years old, "very grey and very black," was worth only two dollars to his master. In 1828, twenty-one-year-old Samuel was listed as worth thirty dollars for his return.

In 1804, William Kirkland lost three female slaves: Jenny, who was about thirty-five to forty years old, and her two daughters, Docia, fifteen years old, and Elsae, who was twelve. The three together were worth thirty dollars.

Sometimes the worth was not listed. In 1805, Stephen Lloyd and Charles King advertised for a mulatto couple who fled. They were about thirty years old, and another slave was believed to have been with them. "A handsome Reward" was offered for their capture. John Faucett offered a "liberal compensation" for the capture of Griffin in 1840.

The comparative value of slaves to implements, animals and other materials on the farm can often be discovered in slave ads. Stephen "took a Black Mare, heavy with soal [foal], without shoes, 5 years old last spring, one hind foot [illegible] to the [illegible] her [illegible] hangs to the left side, a switch tail; she is well formed, about 13 hands 3 inches high. He has carried with him a good bridle, with plated bits, a horsewhip, &c. He is an artful, cunning fellow…I will give the above Reward [$15] to any person who will secure him, so that I get him and the Mare again; and should they be taken up separately, I will give Ten Dollars for the Negro Fellow, and Five for the Mare, on the delivery of them."

Some ads reveal much about the owners themselves. Jefferson Homer, of Orange County, offered ten dollars for his slave, who ran away with no provocation, dead or alive.

In Carteret County, an ad was published by William Bourden in 1778 for "the negro wench" Nan, a dark, eighty-year-old slave, "bred upon Trent," who was valued at $80. In 1790, Peter and the sailboat and the two sails he stole were valued at five pounds. In 1800, "very black" sixteen- or seventeen-year-old Merium was worth $10. Sharp, who was "very sensible" and "well-acquainted with [the] boating and Farming business," along with Jim, who was "surly" and missing some toes, together were worth $20 in 1814, according to William Borden (or Bourden). John—a goliath of a man, standing at six feet five or seven inches high, with thick lips and bushy hair— was worth $50 in 1816, while in the same year, Sam, who was a foot shorter but played the fiddle, was valued only at $25. Twenty-eight-year-old Esther, who was straight and well made and yellow-complexioned, was worth $20 in 1822. In that same year, Cuff, David and Moses ran off with another group of slaves, probably heading to the "Northern States." Their owner, Rebuen Davis, offered $100 for their return. Gloster, who escaped the salt works on Cape Lookout in 1823, was worth $10 if captured in Carteret County and $20 if apprehended outside of the county.

Some ads reveal a sense of compassion. In 1799, Tom ran away from his Chatham County servitude and probably hid among other slaves in Waynesborough. Twenty-two months later, his owner placed an ad offering a reward for his return but also noting that if Tom would return home on his own free will, all would be forgiven.

FIFTY DOLLARS REWARD,
WILL be given for the apprehension and delivery in Newbern Jail of my
Negro Men HUGH and JIM. They ran away from my house in Beaufort,
about ten days ago.—Hugh was raised on Mr. Gaston's Plantation on
Brices Creek, and I expect both of them are dodging about in the bushes
at that place. Hugh is about 28 years old, 5 feet 8 or 9 inches high, is
not a very dark negro, is trim built, with very thick lips. He wears a long,

blue cloth coat occasionally. He has a pass written by my daughter, dated about two weeks ago, to go to Neuse and return, which he will probably show if interrogated [sic]. Jim is a black negro, about 25 years old, about 5 feet 6 inches high, and thick set. He was raised by Mrs. Thompson, in Beaufort, and has a wife at James T. Jones' plantation, on Clubfoot's Creek. Jim has a pass written by me, about two weeks ago, with leave to go to Clubfoot's Creek and return immediately. They have taken a longer tour than I expected, and if they return to me immediately, witout [sic] cost, I will endeavor to sell them to the man they want to live with. When Hugh reads this, he had better reflect on his error, and come home without delay.
JAMES MANNEY.
Beaufort, Nov. 6th, 1831.[83]

Other ads reveal the complexities of runaways.

$200 Reward
WILL [illegible] for the apprehension and delivery to me in this place of my two negro women EVE and SALL. Eve is the wife of Manuel, belonging to Mathew Cluff, and Sall is the wife of old George, also belonging to Mathew Cluff. Eve was seduced away by Manuel in September, 1829, and has since that time been kept out with the assitance [sic] of white persons at or near Elizabeth, and from there to the head of Pasquotank River. She is a low, thick set woman, about 26 or 27 years of age, bushy head of hair, rather thick lips, smooth, dark skin, though not very black and lisps a little when spoken to. I understand she has changed her name to Mary and has a free pass. Sall is a tall, stout woman, smooth skin, about the same complexion and age of Eve.—She was seduced away by old George on the night of the 2nd of this month, on his return from this place to Elizabeth City, where he had been to visit her as usual. His object, no doubt, is to place her with Eve, to be under the protection of that noted villian Manuel and his brothers, who were transported from this County with a view of sending them to New Orleans. I will pay the above reward for both together, with the child or children, of Eve if she has any with her, or $100 for either on delivery.
JOHN WOOD.
Hertford, July 27, 1833.[84]

One last observation is that, before the American Revolution, ads were much longer and composed in very legalistic manner. The king himself was often part of the ad!

BEAUFORT COUNTY, ss.

By THOMAS PEARCE and CHRISTOPHER RESPESS, Esqrs.
Two of his Majesty's Justices of the Peace for said County.

WHEREAS *Complaint aht been made to us by Thomas Bonner and Isaac Patridge, that a Negro Man Slave belonging to the Estate of John Mauel, Esq; deceased, hired by them for one Year, ending in October next, (named ADAM) about 5 feet 10 Inches high, a Country born Fellow, about 38 Years of Age, ran away from them about the 15th of February last, and is supposed to be lurking about, comitting many Acts of Felony.*

These are therefore in his Majesty's Name, to command the said Slave forthwith to surrender himself, and return home to his said Masters. And we do hereby also require the Sheriff of the said County of Beaufort, to make diligent Search and Pursuit after the abovementioned Slave, and him having found, to apprehend and secure, so that he may be conveyed to his said Masters, or otherwise discharged as the Law directs; and the said Sheriff is hereby impowered to raise and take with him such Power of his County as he shall think fit for apprehending the said Slave. And we do hereby, by Virture of an Act of Assembly of this Province concerning Servant and Slaves, intimate and declare, if the said Adam doth not surrender himself, and return home, immdediatley after the Publication of these Presents, and that any Person may kill and destroy the said Slave, by such Means as he or they may think fit, without Accusation or Impeachment of any Crime or Offence for so doing, or without incurring any Penalty or Forfeuitre thereby.

GIVEN under our Hands and Seals, this 9th Day of March, 1775, and in the 15th Year of his Majesty's Reign.

THOMAS PEARCE,
CHRISTOPHER RESPESS.

N.B. The above named Adam was hired by us to to the Complaints, and will warrant the above Proclamation or Advertisement.

MOSES HARE,
JOHN PATTEN,
READING BLOUNT, JUn.
Executors.[85]

Chapter 5

QUAKERS AND THE UNDERGROUND RAILROAD

Mention the Underground Railroad and many people will instantly think of the Society of Friends, better known as the Quakers, who were a major part of this endeavor. Indeed, it is difficult to discuss any part of the Underground Railroad in North Carolina without alluding to a Quaker meeting, family or friend of a Quaker. There were two major regions of Quaker resistance to slavery in North Carolina: the Piedmont around Greensboro, south to the Deep River area and east to Snow Camp, and farther east toward Perquimans County. But there were other Quakers throughout the state who helped as well. Peter, who guided freight boats around the Wilmington port and Cape Fear River, often took fugitives with him. He worked in collusion with two local Quakers, a Mr. Fuller and Mr. Elliot, who both owned oyster sloops. In a biography written by his son, published in 1904 and republished in 1913, the two Quakers are noted as part of the "underground railroad" that ran from North Carolina's coast to Canada. Quaker ship captains, who risked death by the noose if caught, would secret the runaways with no charge to safe havens in the north.[86]

It is easy to believe that Quakers always opposed slavery and were sympathetic toward bondsmen and women. Such was not the case. In fact, Quakers did not allow blacks into their meetings until the 1780s.[87]

Quakers in America, like most of the colonists, were originally in favor of slavery. Many owned slaves and saw nothing wrong with the peculiar institution. But, guided by the ever-progressive Light, sensitivities toward the slaves began to emerge. The first American Quaker protest against slavery

Weeks Slavery Map. Stephen Weeks's 1893 map of Quaker safe havens in North Carolina. *Courtesy of the North Carolina Collection, University of North Carolina at Chapel Hill.*

was in the Germantown meeting in Pennsylvania in 1688. It took a few more years for the antislavery theology to find its way south, but in North Carolina, it found a home first in the Piedmont Quakers, who held few slaves, and eventually east to Quakers who owned more slaves.

Quakers are typically reserved in their theological protests, and so when Quaker John Woolman, traveling through North Carolina, was invited in to stay with families, he would decline to eat their food if the family owned slaves rather than offer a vociferous protest to the owners. He paid the slaves for their services as well. On the other hand, some leading Quakers observed that their fellow Friends who owned slaves were becoming lazy, quite unlike the industrious Friends. By 1776, slave owning or slave trading by North Carolina Quakers was made a disownable offense (one could still take part in the meeting but could not participate in business meetings). This agreement was reasonable, but it raised an important and difficult question: what to do with the slaves?

The complications of slave ownership among Quakers were because of various unobvious situations. Addison Coffin notes that in 1776, the North Carolina Yearly Meeting discussed this issue. What of orphans, minors, old and infirmed slaves who could not support themselves if released and husbands and/or wives who were owned by Quakers who were not in current membership? It was decided that all slavery was to be abolished, no doubt creating problems for both the owners and the recipients of freedom.[88]

There were other issues as well. Quakers are typically quite methodical and yet pragmatic in their morals and logic, so questions arose over how to handle the slavery question. Ethically, should they even be involved in aiding and abetting another's property to run away? Wasn't this like stealing? But what if the runaway came to your house looking for safety? Jesus did not turn away those in need. More than this was the overall question of where the Quakers stood on slavery. Abolition was the cry, but how? Immediate emancipation? Gradual emancipation? Colonization? Resettlement? Gradual emancipation came to be the accepted norm, but for some more radical Quakers, this was not enough.

No matter which method of abolition, if set free, freed slaves could be captured by unscrupulous slave hunters and then sold. With this in mind, some Quakers retained their slaves in a kind of "free-bondage" in which the person was still legally a slave (thus circumventing various laws) but free to move about as if indeed free. In 1808, the North Carolina Yearly Meeting appointed a committee to deal with the problem. Members created a system that allowed the meeting to purchase slaves in order to give them freedom. As Quaker historian Seth Hinshaw noted, "The irony of it all was that Friends thus became legal participants in a system which they abhorred!" Many disagreed with the system, but it remained in place until the Civil War.[89]

By 1824, the North Carolina Yearly Meeting owned over seven hundred slaves. The sheer cost of "upkeep" for so many slaves led to drastic measures. North Carolina Friends were asked to become "owners" of one or more slaves and then take them to free states, usually Ohio or Indiana. Some means of accomplishing this were quite inventive. When the property of Claiborne Guthrie, including his slave, was sold, Quaker Nathaniel Newlin purchased him. When his brother Thomas arrived back from Indiana, Nathaniel deeded the slave to him. Upon arrival in Indiana, the slave was given his freedom.[90]

Such methods were quite altruistic, especially when one considers the initial "cost" and then the logistics of the actual trip to the Northwest. While many Quakers were known for their thrift and solid economic status, taking the time off to travel and stocking the wagon with supplies was still an ordeal. Another tactic was that if Friends from these northern states came back home to visit former neighbors and relatives in North Carolina, then they were asked to take a slave back home with them. Since many North Carolina Quakers had been migrating to what was then called the Northwest since the late 1700s but especially in the early 1800s to escape the culture of slavery in North Carolina, there was quite the potential for moving large numbers of former slaves. Thus began what is commonly referred to among Quakers as the "Over-ground Railroad." Many Quaker families rode in their wagons with one or more blacks tagging along somewhat behind them as they made their way north and west.

There was a preferred way to go about this manumission. George and Delphina Mendenhall, who lived in the Jamestown–Deep River Friends community, gathered slaves in their family units as best as they could and, when ready, took them to Ohio, where they remained with them until the ex-slaves found some occupation with which to provide for themselves. This was much better than others who simply drove north and left the freed slave behind to fend for him or herself. Perhaps as many as two thousand slaves found freedom through this controversial way. But with the increasing influx of slaves, both skilled and unskilled, poor and established, northerners increasingly became frustrated with the Quakers and their abolition. As we have already seen, by the 1830s, some states began making such methods illegal. This more than likely led to the move to the underground railroad tactics, which the North Carolina Quakers *officially* never condoned. But that did not stop some from participating in the effort. Here are the stories of two wealthy Quakers who both inherited slaves.

GEORGE CAMERON MENDENHALL

Before the ratification of the Thirteenth Amendment to the U.S. Constitution brought the end of slavery, there were few ways for a slave to gain their freedom. Some means of emancipation, as we have seen, were initiated by those in bondage. Of course, that meant being so dedicated to escaping their harsh reality that they took emancipation into their own hands and became fugitives. Others were fortunate enough, through various circumstances, to acquire liberty due to the benevolence of their owners. Freedom was occasionally granted through the will of a deceased slave master, and slaves were sometimes allowed to purchase their freedom.

Another means of manumission was by way of the "Over-ground Railroad." The Over-ground Railroad was a method of escaping to a Northern state, or Canada, with not just the permission but also the aid of the slave's master. To bring this about, the owner would arrange a trip to a free state, or arrange for a representative to go, and take along the slave, or slaves, whom the owner intended to free.

However, in the Southern society of the time, where the power elite were white, wealthy and generally slaveholders, doing the right thing did not always come easily. North Carolina law of the day severely restricted slave owners with regard to making their slaves freedmen. Further, if someone was deemed to be soft on the institution of slavery, that person's standing among his peers in the white community could certainly suffer. All of these factors, as well as the conscience of his Quaker heritage, came to bear on George Cameron Mendenhall of Jamestown, North Carolina.

Forty-four-year-old James Mendenhall, George C. Mendenhall's grandfather, uprooted his wife, Hannah, and six of their eight children from their home in Chester County, Pennsylvania, in 1762. They planted new roots in Rowan County, North Carolina, by way of a land grant from colonial proprietor John Earl Granville. The grant was for 204 acres on the Deep River.[91] Today, the county in which the land sets is called Guilford, having been created from parts of Rowan and Orange Counties in 1771.

In 1775, James Mendenhall moved to Georgia. One of his sons, George, was left in charge of the land in Guilford County, as well as the mill that had been established by James. It was George who developed a plan for a settlement, which he named Jamestown in honor of his father.[92] Jamestown still exists today, but some of the original village has been absorbed by the city of High Point.

George Mendenhall and his wife, Judith, were Quakers and farmed the land on which they lived. They had several children, the youngest of whom was George Cameron. George C. was born in 1798, which made him much younger than most of his siblings. In fact, he was twenty years younger than his elder brother Richard, who was born in 1778.[93] Richard's home, Mendenhall Plantation, still stands today on West Main Street in Jamestown, an excellent historic example of an antebellum Quaker home.

George the younger became an attorney and also established a law school close to his home, Telmont, in Jamestown. Like his elder brother Richard, George C. appeared to be a Friend in good standing. Yet a problem arose, when in 1824, at the age of twenty-six, he married Eliza Dunn, a non-Quaker. Marrying outside of the Society of Friends alone was grounds for George C. to be disowned by his fellow Quakers, but Eliza also brought to the marriage slaves, which she had inherited upon the death of her father.[94]

In 1785, emulating the standard set by John Woolman, a New Jersey Quaker, the North Carolina Yearly Meeting of Friends had made the ownership of slaves grounds for disownment. In 1816, convinced of the cruelty of the institution of slavery, the North Carolina Manumission Society was organized. Among its earliest supporters was not only Richard Mendenhall but also, ironically, his younger brother, George Cameron Mendenhall.[95] Although George C. had married outside the Society and in the bargain, acquired slaves, there is no compelling evidence that Richard ever refused to associate with his younger sibling.

In fact, in a statement that is thought to have come from Mary Mendenhall Hobbs, the granddaughter of Richard Mendenhall, Eliza was greatly influenced by young George's older, stately brother and desired to set her slaves free. According to Mrs. Hobbs, "Eliza Dunn Mendenhall sympathized with these views," that is to say the antislavery views of Richard, "and wished her own slaves liberated." Mrs. Hobbs also speculated that had the local Friends not been so hasty in disowning George C., Eliza may have very well become a Quaker herself.[96]

Sadly, in 1826 George lost Eliza after she gave birth to their son, James Ruffin Mendenhall, in 1825. Naturally devastated, George turned his son over to his brother, Richard and his sister-in-law, Mary. Now, Mary was looking after not only her own family of seven children, but she had an infant to care for also.[97]

Six years later, George remarried, which was actually a little unusual for the time. In the nineteenth century, a widower would sometimes marry within a year of the death of his spouse, especially if a child or children were involved. However, George was a professional man with only one child for whom to provide—one that was under the watchful eye and loving care of his brother and sister-in-law. Quick remarriages were more common among those living off the land, with children that needed constant attention.

Interestingly, this time George married a Quaker, Delphina A. Gardner. It should be remembered that her new husband had been disowned by the Friends at Deep River Meeting, so he was not a member of the society. Her home meeting of Cane Creek could have disowned her, but they did not because she went to a women's meeting and apologized for having married outside the society. As a result, when she formally requested the transfer of her membership from Cane Creek Meeting to Deep River Meeting, the transfer was easily granted. Writer and historian Damon D. Hickey once suggested that Delphina's acceptance could have also come as a result of Deep River Quakers' attitudes "mellowing" toward George.[98]

Like a few other Southern slave owners, George Washington and Thomas Jefferson among them, George C. Mendenhall was apparently conflicted about owning slaves. While serving in the North Carolina House of Commons in 1830, he voted for several measures that were friendly to African Americans, both slave and free.[99] Although he could no longer be a practicing Quaker following his first marriage, he had been a member of the North Carolina Manumission Society, as was his brother Richard. Being a slave master, after all, was the result of his marriage to Eliza, not because he had purchased them with the intent of profiting from them.

Something George and his first wife, Eliza, had strongly considered was to devise a plan to free their chattel. Mary Mendenhall Hobbs mentioned years later that the couple felt they needed to see their slaves off safely to a free territory, but beforehand, they wanted to help them find employment, homes and the necessary skills needed to live independent, productive lives. Regrettably, Eliza died before their mission could be accomplished.[100] Why George didn't proceed with the plan despite his wife's death is not entirely clear. This, of course, raised the question: was he keeping them for his own benefit?

It was a certainty, however, that Mendenhall could not protect them if he attempted to confront all of the hurdles necessary to free them in the state. North Carolina law made it extremely difficult and nearly impossible to emancipate slaves within the borders of the state. Also, with the prevailing attitude in the state and in the South generally toward blacks, even a freedman could be returned to slavery if it suited the whims of a white person. All that was required was for a white to claim that a free black was actually a slave, and in many cases, the man or woman would be enslaved by the courts.[101] With this in mind, he may have simply been doing the lesser of two evils. Keeping the slaves may have prevented them from being returned back into slavery into worse situations than they were currently in.

Therefore, it seemed Ohio offered the perfect opportunity for those wishing to set their slaves free because of the Quaker influence that had settled in that state and neighboring Indiana. The settlement in the Midwest by the Friends was a direct result of the existence of human bondage in the South.[102] While Quakers had resided in Guilford, Randolph, Alamance and other surrounding Piedmont counties in great numbers, many of them decided that living within the institution of slavery was so repugnant that they left in droves to Ohio and Indiana. Removing slaves from North Carolina by way of the Over-ground Railroad became the solution many had been looking for. It was this tack that George C. Mendenhall and his second wife, Delphina, decided to take.

Evidence of their decision was discovered in 1975 in the basement of the Logan County, Ohio courthouse. Archivists from Wright State University in Dayton, Ohio, found a book containing court records from as far back as 1818. The book documents the freeing of slaves, beginning in 1838, who had been brought to Ohio, primarily from North Carolina and Virginia, for that express purpose. Among the actions recorded, the book contains the name George C. Mendenhall of Guilford County, North Carolina.[103]

According to the court's records, the procedure to free twenty-eight slaves was taken in Bellefontaine, Ohio, on June 28, 1855, and officially noted on July 2. In the Deed of Emancipation, Mendenhall writes, "This indenture witnesseth that the said George C. Mendenhall in consideration of his own views and of the proper construction of the declaration of independence adopted 4th of July 1776 by the American people, and the further consideration of his own views of the duties of man to his fellow man hath made this deed of emancipation to his said slaves as follows." The document then lists the names, ages and family relationships of the people being freed.[104]

Official census records and family recollections are frankly confusing concerning the number of slaves George Cameron Mendenhall actually owned. He was said to have been among the one or two largest slaveholders in Guilford County. His brother Richard claimed George to have "about one hundred slaves" in 1849. However, the 1850 census showed him possessing thirty-five. Yet Delphina Mendenhall's estate journal, which accounted for all property following George's death, listed thirty-five slaves by name, and that was in 1860—five years after the freeing of twenty-eight people in 1855.[105]

What is certain is that George intended to free his slaves upon his death at the very least. Slightly over a year before Confederate cannons began their bombardment of Fort Sumter in the Charleston Harbor, George C. Mendenhall drowned in the Uwharrie River in Randolph County. It was claimed by one person that when his body was discovered, George was clutching his satchel, which contained papers for the liberation of all of his slaves who still resided in the South. While that statement cannot be verified, Mendenhall did make provisions in his will for all of his slaves to be freed. His will also ordered that his estate should pay for their safe transport to a free territory.[106]

George Cameron Mendenhall was not the perfect example of a Southern abolitionist. He had acquired chattel only through the bonds of marriage but did not follow through with plans for liberating them following his first wife's death in 1826. Why he would delay freedom for the numerous slaves he held for so many years would require guesswork. What seems sure, however, is that by the 1850s, he had become resolute in his determination to see that they were settled in a safe area, under the best conditions possible. Perhaps it was the firm Quaker convictions of his second wife, Delphina, that finally tilted the balance. Maybe it was the influence of his early years as a member of the Society of Friends or the steadying influence of his brother Richard.

Whatever his reasoning, George Cameron Mendenhall is an example of the idiosyncratic nature of many Southern whites. To any number of North Carolina white slaveholders, owning another human being as property was recognized by them as wrong. Yet, by judging African Americans based on their economic worth rather than their humanity, they rated their chattel as necessary. It can be likened to holding a wolf by the ears. Common sense tells you that you have to let go, but self-preservation tells you that you have to hang on.

As the nation was running headlong into a war that put our great democratic experiment in peril, George C. Mendenhall ultimately took an unpopular stand in his native South. Just as the determination to hold on to a doomed way of life was becoming stubborn conviction, he took a different tack. He gave twenty-eight slaves the precious gift of cherished freedom in Ohio in 1855. The rest were freed upon his death in 1860.

JOHN NEWLIN

In 1850, Quaker John Newlin was in charge of forty-two slaves. Neighbors were confused, angry or sympathetic: did he own them, were they waiting freedom or were they working for him? The episode, in historian Carole Watterson Troxler's words, "left a lively and contradictory memory" in the area around Snow Camp and Saxapahaw, both near present-day Graham in the Piedmont of North Carolina.[107]

The story begins many years earlier with Sarah Freeman providing her slaves to John Newlin for construction of his mill in Saxapahaw, specifically a mile-long race from the nearby dam on the Haw River. There was an agreement that, after the job was completed, Newlin would take the slaves north, possibly to Ohio, to freedom. Variations in the story have Newlin doing just that or his son or brother selling them in Fayetteville or that the slaves were emancipated after the Civil War. However, the legal paperwork shows that Newlin took forty-two slaves to Logan County, Ohio, where they were freed in December 1850.

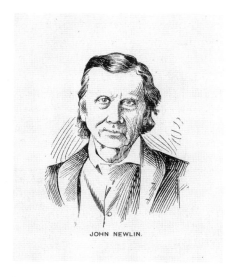

JOHN NEWLIN.

John Newlin. *Courtesy of Alamance County Historical Museum.*

Sarah Freeman acquired the slaves from her first husband, Daniel Faust. They had agreed that their slaves were to be freed and transported to a free state upon his death. But there was a problem. At that time, North Carolina law stated that a slave could only be freed if the owner posted a $1,000 security per slave that guaranteed the slave would not come back to North Carolina. Since this was a prohibitive cost, some slave owners gave their slaves to manumission societies and then gave land to these societies to compensate for the costs of freedom. Sarah retained her slaves for the time being.

She then married again, this time to Richard Freeman, and part of their marriage contract stipulated that neither would lay claim to the other's property. This meant that the slaves from her first marriage remained her property.

When Sarah died in 1839, the matter became even more complicated. Going against his advice, she deeded her slaves to John Newlin. After her death, family from her first marriage contested the will and the matter remained in the courts for years. In the meantime, what was Newlin to do with the slaves that were now in his care? Interestingly, the family of Sarah Freeman/Faust never questioned what Newlin was doing with his slaves. But the community did, and oddly enough, many of his fellow Quakers condemned him as well. At issue was the claim that both Newlin and Freeman hired out the slaves and in essence allowed them the same rights as freedmen. Thus, did Newlin use them for his own gain? Or was he using their labor to pay for their food, lodging and clothing?

In a landmark case, the matter was settled in 1849, and in September 1850, Newlin and the forty-two slaves made the twenty-seven-day trip to Indiana, where Elijah Coffin argued to the Friends Meeting for Sufferings that the ex-slaves be allowed to settle in their area.[108]

LEVI COFFIN

The story of the Underground Railroad in North Carolina begins with a group of Quakers who left their New England home of Nantucket and settled in New Garden, modern-day Greensboro. Elders William and Priscilla Coffin raised their ten children in the values of the Society of Friends. Their home was open to many travelers. The ninth of the children, Levi, was educated somewhat for his day and, in the winter times, taught school. Levi married and moved to his own farm, where he raised seven children, the lone boy being named after his father. While having to farm, he managed to gain a solid education for his circumstances, learning from his dad and attending school when he could.[109]

Young Levi's parents and older sisters moved to Indiana in 1825, and he followed them the year after, settling in Newport. The young Levi's parents and grandparents were both against slavery. But there is a difference between being against slavery and fighting for abolition. In the years of slavery, many Quakers were opposed to the peculiar institution but were not agitating against it.

At the age of seven, the young Levi Coffin witnessed an incident that changed him forever. A chained gang of slaves was being driven like cattle along the Salisbury Road near the Coffin farm. The young and impressionable Coffin was caught off guard by the disturbing sight. Years later, he recalled:

> *My childish sympathy and interest were aroused, and when the dejected procession had passed on, I turned to my father and asked many questions concerning them, why they were taken away from their families, etc. In simple words, suited to my comprehension, my father explained to me the meaning of slavery, and, as I listened, the thought arose in my mind—"How terribly we should feel if father were taken away from us."*[110]

Levi Coffin. Engraving frontispiece as published in the *Reminiscences of Levi Coffin* (1880). *Courtesy of the Friends Historical Collection, Guilford College, Greensboro, North Carolina.*

Another incident sealed the will of young Levi to fight slavery forever, if necessary. At a fish camp on the Yadkin River, one slave, whose master allowed him to fish overnight and sell his catch the next day, was savagely beaten with a stick by someone who thought the slave was overstepping his bounds in selling his fish to a white man.

The young Quaker was fascinated by slaves. At a corn-shucking sponsored by local slave-owner Dr. David Caldwell, neighbors brought their slaves to help. As it happened, a slave dealer from the area came by with a gang of slaves en route to the Deep South for sale. Talking with them as the adults ate dinner, Coffin was moved by their stories and afflictions. He then initiated the rescue of a free-born black man who had been stolen and was being driven to the Deep South for sale.

Runaway slaves often hid in the woods near the Coffin's farm. As did those of most people, the Coffins' hogs ran wild in the woods, and young Levi's chores included carrying sacks of corn out to feed the swine. He knew the area well because he also hunted wild turkey and deer there. So he often stuffed bacon and cornbread in his corn sack and fed the fugitive slaves and listened to their stories. Word got around, and many a night a slave would slip up to Levi's dark room and ask for assistance.

Assistance came from another family member: Vestal Coffin, young Levi's cousin, who joined in the efforts. The two would meet at night in the woods where the runaways hid. Along with them, a trustworthy older local slave named Sol kept on the lookout for kidnapped slaves as well. The kidnapped slave was brought to the woods for an interview to lay plans for an escape. All of this was done in violation of North Carolina law and in proximity to local patrollers and officers of the law.[111]

In his early years, sometimes it was just a matter of convincing the master of a runaway slave that the circumstances of the slave needed to be addressed. In one instance, young Levi's family had taken in a slave mother, Ede, and her sickly baby, who were hiding not far from their farm. Even this very religious act was considered harboring a fugitive slave and was illegal. The mother's master, Dr. Caldwell, was selling her to his son Samuel, the result of which would mean she would be separated from her "husband" (slave marriages were not considered legal at that time). It was a punishment she could not bear, so she ran away. Young Levi went to the farmer's home and argued with scriptural references to the Presbyterian slave owner to persuade him to take her back with no penalty and keep her. The respected doctor was convinced and took her back with no penalty.

Levi Coffin relates another story in which he unwittingly became a slave hunter. One eastern slave owner bachelor neared death and so, as allowed by law, stated in his will that his body servant Jack would gain freedom upon the master's death. As it turned out, relatives contested the will and, knowing that no fair trial would happen in that part of the Tarheel State, Jack worried about what to do. He knew of the Quakers in the New Garden area of the Piedmont who were sympathetic to the causes of slaves. With proper papers in hand, he quietly headed for New Garden in 1821 and found the Coffin home, where he stayed and worked on various farms in the area.

As it turned out, Jack's premonitions were correct: the judge ruled that Jack's owner was not mentally able to make such a decision and so the relatives were to take Jack back as a slave. But they did not know where Jack was. Advertisements were placed in papers across the state, and soon Jack read of his fate. Plans were made by the Coffins to get Jack to the North and freedom. As it turned out, Bethuel Coffin, Levi's uncle, was heading to Indiana to see his children, and though it was dangerous, he agreed to take Jack along since the route he was traveling was sparsely populated.

A local slave named Sam had run away to escape the perpetual beatings of his master. He also found a safe home with the Coffins. The now very angry master heard from someone of a Quaker man heading to Indiana with a black man walking after him. The master, thinking this was his slave, left in pursuit. Young Levi heard about this and worried about his uncle knowing that, should the disgruntled master find Jack with him, he would capture the former slave to get the ransom. Neighbors gave Levi a fast horse, money and goods for travel, and off the young "slave catcher" went.

Levi caught up with the slave owner and rode with him, encouraging him to drink his whiskey while himself abstaining, using deceit but no lies to trick the owner into thinking that he would aid him in capturing his slave. In two days, they caught up to Levi's uncle, and the disgruntled master saw that

Jack was not his escaped slave. When the two returned home, the master then asked Levi to help him hunt for his slave whom he heard was hiding about in the woods near the Coffin farm. Levi agreed but took the master in the very opposite direction from where the slave was hiding. Again, he used trickery to foil the master's plan.

In this story, the former slave Jack walked in the open behind Levi's uncle's wagon along the trail. This could be dangerous: slave hunters could ride up quickly, overcome the "owner" and steal the slave and then rush to sell him in the Deep South. To avoid this, sometimes the "owner" would prearrange a schedule with the would-be runaway. The traveler would ride in the wagon during the day while the slave would hide in the woods at night. In the cover of darkness the slave would then walk the road just covered by the owner and then catch up to where the wagoner had camped for the night. There the slave would eat breakfast and then hide in the woods again for the day. Should a fork occur in the road, a broken limb, bush or other type of sign would be dropped on the left or right side of the road indicating the direction to take. Fording a river was dangerous for two reasons: one, any river could be difficult to cross, and two, the slave would have to ride the wagon across in daylight. The wagon rider would wait for the slave at the river, hide him in the wagon and then take a ferry over the river.[112]

Bands of ruffians often rode these trails looking for runaways. In the summer of 1822, Coffin left North Carolina for Indiana, riding with his brother-in-law Benjamin White. He related that a rough-looking bunch rode up to the wagon and demanded to search it, claiming that they had lost a dog and wondered if the family had taken it. They searched the wagon fiercely but found no dog. They were really searching for runaway slaves, and many wagon trains were subjected to abuse and terror by such bands of thugs.

Coffin recalls the locations of many people who immigrated from the New Garden and Guilford County part of North Carolina to Indiana, and this is helpful in figuring out where potential runaways might be headed. Many from the New Garden area settled in Wayne County, Richmond, Terre Haute, Mooresville, White Lick, Blue River and White Water, Termin's Creek and Honey Creek and areas on the Wabash River in Indiana.

After a year of exploring Indiana, Coffin returned in late 1823 to North Carolina, where he took up teaching and married Catherine White. He taught until 1826, when he and his family moved to Newport, Indiana, where he opened up a mercantile business and eventually a linseed oil company. But he never forgot about the slaves in North Carolina.

Years later, Levi Coffin recalled:

> *Soon after we located at Newport, I found that we were on a line of the U.G.R.R. Fugitives often passed through that place, and generally stopped among the colored people. There was in that neighborhood a number of families of free colored people, mostly from North Carolina, who were the descendants of slaves who had been liberated by Friends many years before, and sent to free States at the expense of North Carolina Yearly Meeting.*[113]

Several things stand out in this recollection. First, Friends had already been liberating some slaves who had made it to the free state of Indiana and resettled there. Second, this set up a destination for other slaves, thus creating a "line" from North Carolina to the Newport, Indiana area that runaways were using. Third, free blacks were taking in these runaways but did not have the means or ingenuity to hide them safely. This is not necessarily a mark against the intelligence of the freed blacks, even though Coffin's remarks could (and have been) be taken that way. People of means could afford large houses with secret rooms, tunnels to other houses or rivers, and the money to make extra meals and offer clothing and shoes to runaways. Fourth, there was no viable system to get slaves to safer territory, such as Canada. No formal network was available, so runaways were being recaptured and taken back home. Fifth, Coffin realized Quakers were avoiding helping out their fellow men and women for fear of legal repercussions or just plain apathy. And once again, he fearlessly stepped in, confronting Quakers and reminding them of their biblical obligations to help their neighbors.

With this in mind, by 1826 into 1827, the Coffin house soon became the destination for many runaways. With so many relatives, friends and neighbors having moved to Indiana, we can assume many connections to the Tarheel State. What route did they take from North Carolina? Coffin provides a few specific routes that could have been used. In the case of Jack, Coffin recalled, "The road they proposed to take was called the Kanawha road. It was the nearest route, but led through a mountainous wilderness, most of the way. Crossing Dan River, it led by way of Patrick Court-House, Virginia, to Maberry's [*sic*] Gap, in the Blue Ridge mountains, thence across Clinch mountain, by way of Pack's ferry on New River, thence across White Oak mountain to the falls of the Kanawha, and down that river to the Ohio, crossing at Gallipolis." Looking back on a failed attempt, Coffin recalled they took the "Kentucky road, crossing the Blue Ridge at Ward's Gap, crossing New River near Wythe Court-House, Virginia, thence by way of Abingdon, crossing Cumberland River near Knoxville, thence over the Cumberland mountains and through Kentucky to Cincinnati, Ohio."[114]

How did they get there? Coffin notes that many fugitives were hidden in wagons, secreted to chambers on steamers or escorted by whites and blacks in the night on various routes known only to a select few. Much of this required money to pay or even bribe folks along the way.

Coffin's definition of the Underground Railroad focuses on the "tracks" from the points of the Ohio River to his home in Indiana and the lines from his house to destinations farther north. There could be several different lines to the next depots, and the line taken depended on where suspected pursuers were. Conductors were always on standby for the next slave running toward freedom. A "train" would arrive at his door in the night, a gentle knock would awaken him and the travelers, typically women and children on the two-horse wagon, would come in and warm up, have a meal and wait, nervously, for the next train. He received passengers at least once a week. Sometimes as many as fifteen or more would be staring at him, frightened, as he opened his door in the night. Most were in need of clothes and shoes, and women in the area formed sewing societies to make new clothes for the destitute runaways. Many had been on the run for months, especially in times when the North Star could not be seen, and were filthy and starving; some were even described as being near wild. Most refused to give their real names, and those who did often received new names for the rest of their journey. Many were understandably reluctant to give details concerning their plight while in slavery.

From Coffin's descriptions, it becomes clear that many slaves simply aimed north, followed the North Star at night when it could be plainly seen and stayed in the woods rather than on roads, lest they be discovered. This information indicates that while some followed wagons, staying near well-beaten paths and roads, others traversed through fields and brambles, over streams and up mountains, following the North Star to where it led, hoping against hope that it led to freedom.

It is clear from Coffin's recollections that his work on the Underground Railroad was well known in Newport, and it is also clear that his reputation as a conductor was known in other states. Coffin received threats from both locals and from people in other states. Threats arrived warning that his business and house would be burned to the ground or, worse, that the whole town would be destroyed. Most locals, however—perhaps out of respect, or because of his wealth and influence in Newport—left him alone. Friends and sympathizers backed Coffin, and slave hunters knew they had best follow the

This iconic 1893 painting by Charles T. Webber, now located in the Cincinnati Art Museum, reveals the traditional image of the Underground Railroad. *Public domain.*

law or, better, stay away from Coffins altogether. Slaves from as far away as Mississippi and Alabama—indeed, all over the South—found their way to Coffin's door. This was a testament to his reputation and the safety of the route that went from his house north to freedom.

In 1847, Coffin moved to Cincinnati, where he thought his work in the Underground Railroad would end. Instead, he found incompetence in the black community when it came to harboring fugitives and getting them to safety and lack of courage in whites who supported abolition in voice but not in action. Most were afraid of the intimidation of proslavery people, public attacks against their character or, even worse, physical harm. White and black workers in the Underground Railroad in the Cincinnati area needed a leader, and Coffin proved worthy of the title.

What is often little understood in tales of the Underground Railroad is the cost. Coffin recalls that it took ten dollars to hire a team of horses from a local German livery who asked no questions. Some nights several teams were needed to move slaves from one station to the next. Often freed blacks would do the driving; other times whites held the reins. On the journey, the teams had to be fed and the drivers (and slaves) boarded and fed. Local women made clothes and shoes were purchased, but these required some sacrificial investment as well. Sometimes slaves saved up money to help before embarking on their journey. Some made baskets on the side, sewed for people in the communities or tended gardens when not working on the plantations or worked on their Sundays off to accumulate modest sums to assist in their escape. When staying in stations or hiding among freed black communities, they would do chores or help the families.

While the work was serious and fraught with danger, Coffin had a sense of humor. He relates this story about one trip to Newport, Indiana:

> *Just before reaching Newport we came to another toll-gate, kept by an old man named Hockett, lately from North Carolina. He had lately been placed here as gate-keeper, and I was not acquainted with him. I halted, and said to him: "I suppose you charge nothing for the cars of the Underground Railroad that pass through this gate."*
>
> *"Underground Railroad cars?" he drawled, sleepily.*
>
> *"Yes," I said; "didn't they give thee orders when they placed thee here to let such cars pass free?"*
>
> *"No," he replied; "they said nothing about it."*
>
> *"Well, that's strange. Most of the stockholders of this road are large stockholders in the Underground Railroad, and we never charge anything on that road. I am well acquainted with the president of this road, and I know that he holds stock in our road. I expect to see him to-day, and several of the directors, and I shall report thee for charging Underground Railroad passengers toll."*
>
> *The gate-keeper seemed much confused, and said that he knew nothing about the Underground Railroad.*
>
> *"Why!" I exclaimed, with apparent surprise, "what part of the world art thou from?"*
>
> *"North Carliny," he drawled.*
>
> *"I thought thee was from some dark corner of the globe," I said, and handed him the money, which I had been holding in my fingers during the conversation, and which was but a trifle. I then started on, but had not gone more than a few rods, when the gate-keeper called to me, and asked: "Is your name Levi Coffin?"*
>
> *"Yes," I replied, "that is my name," but did not check my team, lest he should follow me and give back the money. I had had my sport with him, which was all I wanted.*[115]

In 1856, Levi Coffin sold his store and opened a boardinghouse. His income dropped, but he still worked in the Underground Railroad. He had a special wagon constructed for the purpose. While of the size that would normally carry four slaves, it was outfitted with springs that allowed for six passengers and once it carried eight, although the load was difficult for the one horse. It was rigged with curtains that could be tightly closed to prohibit people from looking in. Neighbors called it the Underground Railroad car, and his horse was called the locomotive.

At the same time, he worked among the poor of the freed blacks in Cincinnati, who were neglected by the whites. Coffin saw no distinction between races and believed all souls were of the same origin.

According to Coffin, when the Civil War began in 1861, the Underground in the North began to wane into the next year, as slaves could now defect to Northern troop lines. Also, it was becoming a more open, indeed "aboveground" railroad in the North.[116] Coffin could even send some slaves northward on a real train—by night, anyway. In 1862, Coffin toured the camps of contraband slaves—slaves who had been abandoned by their owners and left to starve and were in the control of Union troops. He then began organizing aid to these ex-slaves from friends and business acquaintances. He helped with schools and supplies and served as impromptu nurse and in other capacities as well. Some contraband camps numbered in the thousands: disease and starvation was rampant in many. Soon colonies of freedmen were developing in the South, several off the coast of North Carolina on the Outer Banks. Coffin was one of the delegates from Cincinnati who served and advised for the newly developed Freedman's Bureau in 1863. He even organized Freedman's Aid societies in London and Birmingham, England.

Looking back over his thirty years of service, a humble Coffin recalled that he had helped deliver well over three thousand slaves to freedom. He died in Avondale, near Cincinnati, Ohio, on September 16, 1877.

ADDISON COFFIN

Addison Coffin, son of Althea Fluke and Vestal Coffin of Greensboro, was born on January 22, 1822, and was the cousin of Levi Coffin. Writing before 1897, he recalled his involvement in the Underground Railroad. His father died in 1826 but was involved in the antislavery movement before his death, first in a legal case. Addison claims that his father, Vestal, originated the Underground Railroad in 1819.[117]

Addison recalls the story of John Dimery as part of the inspiration for his role in the Underground Railroad. John was freed by his master in the lower part of the state, and he then married a free woman. They came to New Garden (modern-day Greensboro), where they settled down and bore and raised seven children. John's former owner died, and two of his sons came looking for John. They found him and tried to take him back. Addison's father, Vestal, and neighbor Isaac White intervened and confronted the two thieves. During the squabble, John escaped to the woods and hid until he could be placed on the Underground Railroad for Indiana, where he worked for two years, sending money back home for his family until they could join him there.[118]

Addison notes, "There was more of this kind of business done at that period than assisting real fugitive slaves."[119] Intervening in legal issues and prohibiting kidnappers from stealing freed slaves was more the role than actually providing safe travel for runaways. In 1772, North Carolina Friends released their slaves, as did many Methodists in the Piedmont of North Carolina. Freedom was one thing, but *staying* free was difficult, as heirs tried to reclaim their slaves and kidnappers roamed about looking for former slaves to steal and sell for profit. Addison notes that thousands of freed slaves fled north through the Virginia mountains rather than heading more westward to Kentucky.

After Addison's father died, there was a brief lull in aiding the slaves as Addison and his siblings helped their mother. In 1833, the destitute widow and her children rode to Indiana, following many Quakers who fled the slavery South for greener pastures. However, she came back within a year and began work at New Garden Boarding School. In 1835, Addison's desire to help slaves was inspired by the story of Solomon, as related in the introduction of this book. Addison had a keen sense of discernment, and he could read faces quite well. If slaves came to him and did not look as if they could keep the secrets of the Underground Railroad or endure the arduous journey, they were returned to their masters. The Coffins never actively searched out slaves; that would have violated Quaker morals. Instead, they only assisted those who came to their doorstep seeking help.

One trick used to aid fugitives was to give them fake papers. Arch Curry was a free black in the New Garden vicinity, but he, like other free blacks, had to carry papers to prove his status if stopped by whites. After he died, his widow, Vina, would give these papers to fugitives who looked much like Arch, and then they would be coupled with Quakers moving to Indiana. If stopped, the papers were produced and the black man was judged as free and allowed to accompany the white Friends on their journey. Upon arrival, the papers were given back to Levi Coffin, who then returned them to New Garden in North Carolina, where the ruse was employed again. Addison Coffin estimates this was done at least fifteen times.[120]

Another trick introduced by Vestal Coffin was for slaves to make their bodies appear afflicted so they would not be sold on the auction block. Bandages or hot burdock root could be applied in such a way as to make the joints and appendages swell so that it was feared the slave had dropsy, rheumatism or other afflictions.[121]

It is not clear how long Addison worked or how involved he was in the Underground Railroad in North Carolina. His memoirs are often vague in details. He left for an adventure in 1843 that took him to Indiana, then to New Orleans by riverboat and then back to Indiana, where he stayed with the Alfred Hadley family (who hailed from the Piedmont area) and worked on the Underground Railroad there. How he worked or what his role was is not mentioned.

During the Civil War, Addison and others in Indiana aided both Union and Confederate troops who fled the battlefields. Union soldiers would come to him for counsel and aid. It should come as no surprise that he aided mostly the Confederate deserters from Tennessee and North Carolina. The farmers in Hendricks County, Indiana, where Coffin resided, who came from the South provided safe havens for deserters and those evading conscription. North Carolina had the highest number of troops in the Civil War and also the highest number of deserters. These Southern soldiers provided much of the farm labor in Ohio, Indiana and Illinois from 1863 to 1864, replacing those Northern farmers who had been called into service.[122]

The Underground Railroad did not close after the Civil War. Many southerners hoped that slavery would be reinstated or recompensed for them by the government, thus they still kept their freed slaves in bondage. Coffin recalls that one freed slave requested that he go back to North Carolina and retrieve his family. Even though the war had ended, hostilities remained, so the trip would be dangerous. Relatives and friends warned Addison not to go back, but go he did. He returned with fifty slaves, most of whom were women and children.[123]

From this point, Addison Coffin changed his mission to helping white immigrants (and a few blacks) leave the devastated South for points north and west. After many extensive travels throughout the world, he died at his daughter's home in Amo, Indiana, on April 16, 1897.

Chapter 6

WILLIAM STILL

I t could be said that no person did as much for slaves escaping the shackles of property than William Still, with the exception of perhaps Harriet Tubman. Working as he did as the secretary and, later, chairman of the General Vigilance Committee of the Pennsylvania Society for the Abolition of Slavery, Still was in a unique position to assist slaves on their way to a free state or Canada

As runaways came through Philadelphia, Still conducted interviews. While conducting the interviews, he was dedicated to taking fairly meticulous notes. These sessions with slaves who were pursuing their cherished liberty served as the basis of his book, originally published in 1872, that chronicled the multitudes of men, women and children whom he aided on their way to self-determination. Though Still was never a slave himself, there can be no doubt that he often heard about the horrors of that institution from his parents.

William Still was born to former slaves Levin and Charity Still on October 7, 1821. He was the last child born to the couple, who had seventeen children before him. Still was raised in New Jersey, and even though his education was intermittent, he was a voracious reader. Young William worked for his father chopping wood and transporting it to a local sawmill. While on the road to the sawmill, he consumed chapter after chapter of history and geography from (and often memorized portions of) the *Young Man's Own Book*.[124]

In 1844, William trod the same path as some of his siblings and moved to Philadelphia. He had high hopes that life would be good for a young

African American in Philadelphia. However, he quickly encountered discrimination and prejudice not unlike that which he had experienced in his native rural New Jersey. At first, life looked bleak for Still, as all he could get for work were low-paying, unskilled jobs.

His fortunes took a turn for the better when he was hired by Mrs. Elwyn to be the groundskeeper at her stylish estate in Philadelphia, and at a good salary.[125] Mrs. Elwyn was actually Mrs. E. Langdon Elwyn, who lived with her daughter on West Penn Square. She was a widow of significant wealth and high social standing in the city.[126]

Mrs. Elwyn had an impressive library, and it didn't take long for William to take notice. Seeing the young man's interest, she helped him select books that would continue to develop his keen mind. He borrowed the books, read them and worked on improving his writing skills.

Portrait and signature of William Still. *Wikimedia.*

By 1847, however, Mrs. Elwyn had moved from Philadelphia to live in New York, but with a glowing reference from the widow, Still gained employment with a gentleman named William Wurtz. Mr. Wurtz was a retired merchant who lived on Walnut Street.[127] While in Mr. Wurtz's employ, William saw an ad in the window of the Pennsylvania Anti-Slavery Society for a part-time janitor and mailroom clerk.

The first American Anti-Slavery Society was formed in Philadelphia in 1834. Others followed quickly, and by the late 1830s, antislavery societies had formed all over the nation. Associated with these antislavery societies were Executive Committees and General Vigilance Committees. The purpose of these latter committees was not only to expand the cause of abolition but also to assist slaves as they escaped the bonds of chattel labor. The vigilance committees were headed by blacks, who worked closely with the executive committee to seek the financial resources necessary to aid runaways as they made their way North.[128]

After seeing the notice for employment, Still decided to apply and was hired.[129] In 1852, partially because of the Fugitive Slave Act of 1850, the society formed the General Vigilance Committee. Still served as the committee's secretary and, eventually, its chairman.[130]

With his newfound duties, William set about keeping his accounts of the slaves that the General Vigilance Committee aided. The vast majority of the runaways the committee helped were from the border states of Kentucky, Maryland, Delaware and Virginia. However, there were also scores of slaves who escaped the clutches of the Deep South. Mr. Still documented slaves who were fleeing their sordid lives from as far away from Philadelphia as New Orleans.

In addition to the massive amount of border state escapees, William Still detailed several runaways from North Carolina. Their stories include a female slave and her two sons, who were in Philadelphia with their master, as the North Carolinian was on his way to New York; a man who escaped the yoke of a former governor of North Carolina and who hid in the woods and swamps for ten months until he could be delivered by ship to Philadelphia; another escapee who would later become a member of North Carolina Reconstruction legislature; and numerous other harrowing escapes from plantations in the Tarheel State.

In the sweltering Philadelphia heat of July 1855, William Still was brought a note by a young African American boy. It was an urgent message suggesting that he get to the Bloodgood's Hotel as quickly as possible because there were three slaves at the hotel with their master, bound for New York. The information was probably the result of an observation of a member of the society or committee or, at the very least, a sympathizer of their efforts.

The master, as it turned out, was John Hill Wheeler of North Carolina, who had received an appointment from President Franklin Pierce as the United States minister to Nicaragua. Wheeler had been active in state politics since after receiving his license to practice law in 1827. He had been elected to the state's legislature, ran for a seat in Congress, served as the superintendent of the Charlotte branch of the U.S. Mint and had twice been considered as the Democratic nominee for governor, only to see the nomination go to someone else.[131] Mr. Wheeler and party were passing through Philadelphia on their way to New York. Feeling confident that he had his slaves' loyalty, Wheeler had brought a female slave, Jane Johnson, and her two young sons with him.

Arriving at the hotel, Still and another abolitionist, Passmore Williamson, discovered that the Wheeler group had already boarded a ferry. Like

John Hill Wheeler, slave owner and U.S. minister to Nicaragua. *Wikimedia.*

JANE JOHNSON.

Jane Johnson, escaped slave, circa 1871. *Wikimedia.*

Still, Passmore Williamson was a committed abolitionist. He was born a Quaker in 1822 in Chester County, Pennsylvania. Through his zeal, he had become the only white member of the Acting Committee of the Vigilance Committee.[132]

Realizing that time was of the essence, Williamson and Still rushed on board the ferry, where they finally found Jane Johnson and her two sons. The men immediately informed Johnson that, according to Pennsylvania law, she and her two young children were entitled to their freedom.

John Wheeler, who had been seated nearby, protested that Jane Johnson had no desire to leave his service. Wheeler persistently tried to get her to declare that she did not wish to seek her freedom, to which she ultimately replied, "I am not free, but I want my freedom—ALWAYS wanted to be free!! But he holds me."[133]

Enough time had passed that the ferry was just about to depart, and the time for Jane Johnson to decide whether to follow William Still and Passmore Williamson to freedom was at hand. One of the men, either Still or Williamson, encouraged Johnson and her two boys to accompany them off the ferry. Bystanders who were sympathetic to the slaves' plight also prompted her to take her sons and go. Finally, her decision made, Johnson and her sons began walking with Still and Passmore toward the stairway that would take them ashore.[134]

It was then—obviously realizing that the slave he had been so sure would not desert him was about to claim emancipation for herself and her sons—that the slave master attempted to physically restrain Johnson. At that point, Passmore Williamson took Wheeler and bodily set him aside. The only other voice of dissent was someone Still assumed to be a slave owner himself, who proclaimed that Still and Williamson were stealing someone's property.

Once Jane Johnson and her sons were on the wharf, they were escorted by William Still and Passmore Williamson to Front Street, where a carriage was hailed. While Johnson and her boys were being loaded into the carriage,

Williamson and the slaveholder, John Wheeler, engaged in a very lively argument concerning the legality of what was being done. However, the carriage took the freed mother and sons on to Tenth Street, where they were left at a safe house. It was only then, among the hospitality of helpful people and away from the bustle of Philadelphia's wharf, that Johnson finally allowed herself to contemplate freedom—real freedom for herself and her sons!

Wheeler, of course, pressed charges and was determined to get back what he considered to be his property. However, Williamson, who was named in the writ of habeas corpus, had not been told the whereabouts of Johnson and her children once they had left the wharf in the carriage. Therefore, when he answered that he did not know where they were, he was, in fact, being truthful. In the end, Passmore Williamson was imprisoned for contempt of court, but nothing more. William Still had also been named in the writ, but he was acquitted.

In a way, the trial was an odd scene because the United States district attorney who was prosecuting the case on behalf of Wheeler and the federal government was obligated to try to get Johnson and sons returned to Wheeler by way of the Fugitive Slave Act of 1850. The defense attorney for Jane Johnson was just as adamantly declaring the laws of the state of Pennsylvania, under which Johnson claimed her freedom, to be sacrosanct.

To add to the drama, Jane Johnson testified at the trial. It was an audacious move, considering the United States district attorney swore he would take her, and a United States marshal was present with a warrant, plus a force of deputy marshals. Meanwhile, Pennsylvania state officials were just as determined that Johnson would not be apprehended. People were abuzz at the prospects of an altercation between the federal and state forces when Jane Johnson attempted to leave. However, the excitement was ultimately unfounded. After her testimony and being granted her freedom, Johnson was escorted to an awaiting carriage. Accompanied by an official of the Pennsylvania Anti-Slavery Society and a police officer, she was taken back to her house of refuge, her freedom never again questioned.[135]

Another narrative by Still involved a slave from North Carolina named William Jordan who also went by the alias "William Price." Jordan had been the slave of a former governor of North Carolina for only twelve months before his escape. However, as to the identity of the governor, for reasons unknown, there seems to be some confusion. An attempt to untangle the details follows.

The governor to whom Jordan was bonded is identified in Still's narrative as "Governor Badger, of North Carolina." Ownership of Jordan was also delineated by Still by saying, "Previous to coming into the governor's hands, William was held as the property of Mrs. Mary Jordan." The account further distinguishes Mary Jordan as being the third wife of the governor. Also, a reading of Still's entry on Jordan may leave the reader with the understanding that William was the slave of the current North Carolina governor. These four points are the ones about which there appears to be some confusion, and some attempt to reconcile these points is necessary before the entire account of William Jordan can be related.[136]

First, North Carolina has never had a governor by the name of Badger. However, George Edmund Badger served as a judge, briefly served as United States secretary of the navy under presidents William Henry Harrison and John Tyler and also served as United States senator from North Carolina from 1846 to 1855. He signed North Carolina's Ordinance of Secession in May 1861, in spite of being a defender of the Union until Lincoln's call for troops in April of that year. Badger, who was born on April 17, 1795, died on May 11, 1866, following an illness of a few days.

George Edmund Badger was indeed married three times, although none of his marriages were to Mary Jordan. As a matter of fact, his third marriage, the marriage to which William Still specifically refers, was to Delia Haywood Williams. As chronicled earlier, Still took notes as he conducted his interviews with the slaves the Vigilance Committee assisted. Perhaps he misunderstood William Jordan, perhaps Jordan misspoke or, still yet, maybe Still misinterpreted his own notes as he was editing and compiling them before publication in 1872. All these years later, it is hard to say.

One possibility is that the governor to whom Still refers may actually be Governor John Branch. Branch served as North Carolina's chief executive from 1817 to 1820, and he was married twice. His second marriage was to Mary Eliza Bond, née Jordan.[137] As a result, the governor Still refers to in his

George Edmund Badger, U.S. senator from North Carolina, but never governor. *Courtesy of the State Archives of North Carolina.*

95

narrative about William Jordan could be former governor John Branch, rather than George Edmund Badger.

One last rather conflicting point is that when reading Still's account of William Jordan, it leaves an impression that the governor in question would have been the current governor. Since Jordan arrived in Philadelphia in 1855, North Carolina's governor then would have been Thomas Bragg, who six years later would become the Confederacy's attorney general. However, again the point of contention becomes Mary Jordan. Bragg only had one wife throughout his life, and she was Isabelle Cuthbert.[138]

In spite of these contentious points, William Jordan's story is a compelling one. William apparently came to the governor by way of his marriage to Mary Jordan. The treatment of William and his fellow slaves on the plantation was not unlike that of many others throughout the South. In his story to Still, William suggests that floggings were not as common on their estate as might have occurred on other plantations. However, clothing was not given out generously, and they were under constant scrutiny by the overseer and the governor.

William Jordan had a wife but had been separated from her, as was often the case throughout the antebellum South. Based on Still's narrative, it was William's understanding that when he and his wife had been split apart, he had been promised the opportunity to "over-work," as the story states it, and make the two-hundred-mile journey once or twice a year to visit his wife. Yet once he was parted from his wife, it was made clear to him that there was no way he was going to be allowed to visit her.

It was then that William decided that he would make his escape and live in the wilderness if necessary. This is exactly what William did. He took to the woods and swamps and managed to live for ten months, with the constant danger of wild animals and venomous snakes all around him.

In order to subsist, William would leave the cave in which he hid and strike out at night to neighboring plantations, where friends might give him whatever they could. Occasionally, he would take a pig or anything else he could use as food. During these ten long months, William had a friend, although the narrative never relates exactly who the friend was, who was on the lookout for a means of exodus to the North.

Finally, aided by one whom the story refers to only as "Captain F," William made his way to Wilmington, Delaware, where he met Thomas Garrett, an antislavery activist. Garrett lived in Wilmington and was an important link on the seagoing Underground Railroad. Several of his letters can be seen in Still's book, which serve as correspondence on the slaves who passed from

Wilmington to Philadelphia. His activities were considered so important in fact, that he is the inspiration for a Quaker named Simeon Halliday in Harriet Beecher Stowe's *Uncle Tom's Cabin*.[139]

According to a letter written by Thomas Garrett to William Still, William Jordan was keen to make his way farther north as quickly as possible—and justifiably so. Therefore, Garrett gave William boots and enough money to pay for his passage to Philadelphia.[140]

The extent to which slaves would go to secure their freedom may be illustrated in another escape narrative that William Still relates about two men from Wilmington, North Carolina, who made their way to Philadelphia via a schooner that was hauling turpentine. A twenty-one-year-old mulatto, Abraham Galloway, and twenty-three-year-old Richard Eden arrived in Philadelphia probably sometime in 1857. Abraham, referred to as "Abram" in Still's account, and Richard were bleeding from their skin pores when first interviewed by Still and other members of the Vigilance Committee. The bleeding was the result of being confined to the hold of the ship with the fumes of the turpentine for the entire voyage. Still recorded, "The blood was literally drawn from them at every pore in frightful quantities."[141]

Galloway was a master builder and, as a result, could earn rather good wages if permitted by his owner, Milton Hawkins (or Hankins).[142] Milton was the Wilmington and Manchester Railroad's chief engineer and, according to Galloway, "was a man of good disposition."[143] He allowed Galloway to hire himself out, but in return, the slave was ordered to pay his owner fifteen dollars a month. That was in addition to buying his own clothing, paying his own medical bills and a head tax of fifteen dollars a year.

Milton was only seven years older than Galloway and had owned his slave since he was very young. He lived in Smithville, today called Southport, with his widowed mother. His father had been a Methodist minister and was killed when a boat capsized off Oak Island.

Richard Eden's owner was a widow, Mrs. Mary Loren (or Ormes).[144] Much less is known about Mary than is known about the background of Galloway's master, but Richard indicates that she was a kindly person. She would tend to Richard with care when he was sick. Eden was a barber and had both male and female clients. Mary owned twenty slaves, all of whom were hired out, with the exception of two small children. However, Richard had to pay his master $12.50 each month, pay his own medical expenses, buy his own clothing and pay a state head tax of $0.25 per month.

For his part, Galloway was having struggles paying his monthly allotment to his master due to the arrival of Irish and German immigrants to the

Wilmington, North Carolina area. Galloway knew full well that if he became an economic hardship on Milton, good disposition or not, that putting him on the market for sale could mean that he might wind up in service much deeper in the South, where escape to freedom would be much harder and the threat of being worked to death more likely.[145]

Meanwhile, Eden was having problems of his own. He had married a free woman, a violation of North Carolina law at the time. If charged, he could be sentenced to a penalty of thirty-nine lashes of the whip and imprisonment if the judge wished to administer punishment to the fullest extent of the law.

Galloway had decided that even though he had never suffered physically under his master, slavery was wrong. Eden felt it was simply a matter of time before he was charged with the crime of being married to a free woman. With both men having the freedom to come and go pretty much as they wished, they knew each other well. After much earnest conversation, they decided that their best course was to attempt an escape to the North by way of the best means possible.

After carefully locating the captain of a Wilmington, Delaware schooner, they agreed on a plan. They learned when the ship would set sail, but they knew full well that it was state law that all ships heading North were to have their cargo holds smoked before leaving port. The express purpose of the smoking was to force out of hiding—or kill—any slaves attempting to run away.

Galloway and Eden had devised a masterful plan to try to foil the smoking of the hold by using a bladder of water and wet towels, which could be held to their noses, and donning silk oilcloth shrouds, which would be tied around their waists. When the hour of departure arrived, it was the good fortune of both men that the cargo hold was not smoked. However, they still suffered from the loss of blood due to their confinement with the barrels of turpentine.

Both men were aided in their escape from Philadelphia to eventually arrive in Canada. However, Abraham Galloway returned to North Carolina during the Civil War to fight and act as a spy for the Union. After the war, he remained in North Carolina and was elected to the state senate. Regrettably, he was to serve in that capacity only a short while, dying on September 1, 1870, in Wilmington.[146]

Miles White, who was twenty-one years old and from Elizabeth City, is also mentioned in William Still's notes. Four North Carolina men escaped aboard a schooner to Wilmington, Delaware, in 1856 and were aided by Thomas Garrett to Philadelphia and the awaiting Vigilance Committee.

They were Major Latham, forty-four; William, the only name given for him, forty-two years old; Henry Gorham, who was thirty-four; and Andrew, the only name written in Still's notes, twenty-six years of age.[147]

One North Carolina slave who evaded capture to make it to Philadelphia was Harry Grimes. Harry had been sold three times in his life; the last time to Jesse Moore, who, according to Grimes, was a drunk and a crude taskmaster. He related one story to Still about a fellow slave in Moore's charge who tried to escape but was later caught. The slave, whose name was Richmond, had his feet split for his efforts.

Grimes was the victim of one of Moore's abuses when he made his run for freedom. Moore had not been satisfied with the amount of work done one day and asked why more had not been accomplished. When Grimes told him he had worked, his master plunged a knife into his neck in a drunken rage. Moore told the overseer to get some rope, while Moore got a gun. That's when Grimes cried, "Masa, now you are going to tie me up and cut me to pieces for nothing."[148]

Harry Grimes then told his master he would leave him and let him shoot him rather than be tied and cut to pieces. It was at that point that Moore told him to go! Grimes began running as Moore "snapped both barrels at me."[149] Moore set his dogs out after Grimes, but according to the slave, the dogs would not pursue him because he had been the one feeding them. Finally, the master and the overseer hunted him with horses, but they could not track him without the aid of the dogs.

Grimes spent the next seven months hiding in the hollow of a poplar tree or a cave. He subsisted on bread, potatoes and roasting ears. He also killed a poplar leaf moccasin that was attempting to use the same poplar tree that Grimes was using for shelter. In order to obtain the freedom he so desperately sought, he had to leave behind a wife and eight children.[150]

Still also made note of another slave from North Carolina named Jacob Brown. His arrival was included with several others who had made their way by ship to Philadelphia sometime in 1856. Among the brief notations made about Brown, Still says, "At the age of twenty, he resolved he would run away if it cost him his life."[151]

One final North Carolinian of whom William Still made note was Dick Beesly. Dick had fled the farm of Richard Smallwood, who, according to Dick, owned 260 slaves in "Wheldon," but it was probably Weldon in Halifax County. Apparently, Smallwood, who Beesly described as a "tough, drinking man," acquired most of his slaves when he married. Still did not expand greatly on Dick's story other than to say he was not sick when he arrived in Philadelphia, he had already been sold three times in his life and that "he was too sharp to be kept in Slavery."[152]

These narratives are the ones in William Still's notes that came from North Carolina. Many, many other slaves fled their fates from Virginia, Maryland and Delaware, which are states that share their borders with Pennsylvania. The Vigilance Committee aided slaves from Washington, D.C.; South Carolina; and well into the Deep South. All of them yearned to live lives that were owned, directed and dictated by no one other than themselves.

Chapter 7

AUSTIN BEARSE, WILLIAM BEARD AND WILLIAM MITCHELL

Not all of the accounts about runaway slaves and the Underground Railroad in North Carolina are about the slaves themselves. As with people like William Still in Philadelphia, those who aided slaves in their flights were instrumental, especially once a slave had made it to a free state. In the North, the individuals who offered a helping hand were members of Vigilance Committees, Abolitionist Societies or Manumission Societies. Often the people who were members of these organizations were from the area in which their committee or society operated. On the other hand, many individuals who tirelessly labored to offer freedom to bonded souls had relocated from slave states to northern locations.

William Beard was a native North Carolinian and, like Levi Coffin, moved to Indiana when the presence of slavery became too much for him to bear. Reverend William M. Mitchell was also born in North Carolina and, for a while, was an overseer on a plantation before also moving north to take up the cause of manumission.

Runaway slaves from the South in general, and North Carolina in particular, seem to have headed to four primary areas of the North in order to seek refuge and to receive support. These areas were Philadelphia, Boston, Ohio/Indiana and New York City. We have already seen the role of William Still of Philadelphia. Another nonnative North Carolinian who was also instrumental in the escape of at least three slaves that boarded ships in the Tarheel State was Captain Austin Bearse of Boston.

Bearse was born in 1808 in Barnstable, Massachusetts. As was the case with many coastal New Englanders, he made a life for himself at sea. From 1818 to 1830, Bearse crewed aboard a variety of ships that plied the waters along the coast of South Carolina, mainly during the winter months. Throughout these winter voyages, it was not unusual for the vessel on which he served to journey up rivers along the coast of the South to haul various kinds of cargo.

Frequently, the cargos they hauled were rice and cotton from the numerous plantations. However, they regularly carried slaves to the Charleston market as well. There were many reasons for slaves to be taken to the market. Sometimes the sales were brought about by the death of the owners and the division of estates. Other reasons for having slaves sold were for the insubordination of the slaves or because the owners were moving either north or west and they felt selling their slaves was easier than transporting them to another location.[153]

Bearse saw as few as two or three slaves aboard ship up to as many as seventy or eighty on their way to the slave market in Charleston. Whatever the reason for taking the slaves to market, or whatever the body count, the assignment sometimes meant the separation of family members with, as Bearse relates, "as little concern as calves and pigs are selected out of a lot of domestic animals."[154]

While Bearse was serving as mate aboard the brig *Milton* out of Boston in 1828, four quadroons, a word commonly used during that time meaning a person of mixed races, were brought on board. Bearse was to take the slaves to New Orleans. While underway, the men told Bearse that they would not live to be slaves in New Orleans. The slaves were turned over to an agent in New Orleans, who later related to Bearse that all four slaves, true to their word, were dead within forty-eight hours. One had even drowned himself by jumping overboard from a steamer he had been assigned to, which was on its way to Belize.[155]

The cries of anguish that Bearse witnessed when families were sold to different owners, and therefore separated forever, embittered him to the institution and made him an enemy of slavery. As a result, he decided to have nothing to do with the support of humans owning their fellow humans, saying, "Because I no longer think it right to see these things in silence, I trade no more south of Mason and Dixon's line."[156]

Bearse first became active in aiding the escape of slaves in 1847. He had docked his ship in Albany, New York, and was made aware of a slave named George Lewis, who had a writ issued against his return to his slave master, who was also his half brother, in Virginia. Captain Bearse managed to pick Lewis up in New York City and safely smuggle him to Boston, where he was reunited with one of his daughters. Eventually, enough money was raised so a representative could go to Richmond, Virginia, where the rest of Lewis's family was purchased and returned to Boston, no doubt to an affectionate reunion.[157]

One North Carolina slave who fled to Boston and to the aid of the Vigilance Committee was Elizabeth Blakesley. A mulatto from Wilmington, Elizabeth secreted herself on board a Boston brig and hid in an area with just two feet eight inches of room. Her master, suspecting she was on the ship, came on board and cried out, "You had better come out! I am going to smoke the vessel!" Which he did, three times with sulphur and tobacco. However, Elizabeth's determination was so strong that she managed to withstand the acrid smoke and arrived in Boston half-frozen and barely able to walk but free.[158]

Twice Bearse was able to deceive crews that had sailed out of Wilmington into thinking that he was some sort of official, and he was able to gain the freedom of two imprisoned slaves on board the vessels. In July 1853, Bearse was the captain of the yacht *Moby Dick*. The Vigilance Committee had received word through some black men on Long Wharf that the brig *Florence*, which was anchored off shore, had a slave in its possession. Captain Bearse and about seven or eight other men sailed out into the harbor and located the *Florence*.

Fortunately, the captain of the brig was on shore attending to some legal matters, so Bearse boarded the ship and demanded of the mate that he release the slave to him. The ship's mate tried to delay by asking for papers but Bearse insisted, found the imprisoned man and took him aboard the *Moby Dick*. While making for shore, the slave changed into a fishing suit so he would not draw attention later. The fugitive told the captain afterward that God had told him the previous evening that someone would set him free the next morning. After the slave was successfully hidden in Boston for a while, he was guided via the Underground Railroad to Canada.[159]

On an evening in September 1854, Bearse made a similar but even more audacious move to set a fugitive slave free. The schooner *Sally Ann*, which had recently sailed out of Wilmington, was anchored in Boston Harbor. There was a slave on board the ship, and Bearse had been led to believe that the captain was eager to get rid of him. However, when Bearse hailed the schooner and asked the crew if they were ready to give up the slave, the answer was, "If you come alongside my vessel, I will send you into eternity—quick!"[160]

So, Bearse sailed into Long Wharf in Boston Harbor and devised a plan. He picked up another member of the Vigilance Committee, who as it turned out was to be the only man on the vessel other than Bearse. As Bearse relates, "Knowing it was soon coming daylight, I had to lay a plot. I took a dozen old hats and coats and fastened them up to the rail in my yacht, which gave me the appearance of having so many men." He then sailed back out to the *Sally Ann* and again demanded the slave, indicating that with his reinforcements, he wanted the slave and that bloodshed should be avoided. The fugitive was given up, and Bearse returned to Boston with him. He was hidden at Bearse's home until he could be safely transported to Canada.[161]

Another essential player in the Underground Railroad in Indiana and Ohio was William Beard. Beard was a native of Guilford County, North Carolina, and a Quaker. Like so many other Quakers of the region, Beard eventually moved to Indiana because of his fierce opposition to slavery. While he lived in Union County, Indiana, he farmed, served as a minister and worked alongside the famed abolitionist Levi Coffin. Popular legend has it that the majority of slaves who went through Coffin's station in Indiana, near Salem, were sent there by Beard.[162]

The ingenuity that Beard, his accomplices and all those who worked on the Underground Railroad exhibited were both creative and constant. As an example, while in Cincinnati, Ohio, after Coffin had moved there in 1847, Beard received from Coffin a female slave who was believed to be under close surveillance. In order to get the girl safely to Beard, Coffin's wife, Katy, devised a fearless plan. The young black lady was dressed in a nurse's uniform and provided with a rag doll to carry. Katy attired herself in a stylish outfit and had the slave girl walk along behind her as they made their way to the house of a coconspirator. The ruse to make the girl appear to be Mrs. Coffin's nursemaid worked, and they arrived without incident. Beard was then able to pick the girl up, whereupon he spirited her away.[163]

In 1844, Beard and Coffin made a trip to Canada to look in on the numerous runaways they had sent there. The two men set out on their mission on September 9, but on their way, they stopped over in several African American villages in Ohio and Michigan. One stop included Detroit, where they looked at schools and visited the families of escaped slaves, and then they crossed over into Canada. William Beard's Underground Railroad accomplishments covered such a wide area and spanned so many years that it is believed the people he aided could have exceeded one thousand.[164]

Another native North Carolinian, the Reverend William M. Mitchell, had a very unique background. Mitchell, like Beard, was born in Guilford

Reverend William M. Mitchell, circa 1859. *Wikimedia.*

County, North Carolina. Mitchell's mother was a Native American, while his father was a free African American. This distinctive combination of parents, however, meant that he was born free. Yet he was indentured for twelve years to a planter. At the end of his indentured term, he became the plantation overseer where he had served his indenture. He labored in this role for five years. It was a five-year span that Mitchell would come to regret due to the cruel punishments he handed out and the families he was responsible for separating.[165]

In 1843, Mitchell, like many other abolitionists before and after him, left North Carolina, moved to a free state and settled in Ross County, Ohio. It is in Ohio that Reverend Mitchell joined the Vigilance Committee and devoted himself to assisting the bonded to the safety of Canada. Mitchell quoted Deuteronomy 23:15–16 in order to justify and make clear his intentions: "Thou shalt not deliver unto his master the servant which is escaped from his master unto thee: he shall dwell with thee, even among you, in that place which he shall choose, in one of thy gates, where it liketh him best: thou shalt not oppress him."[166]

After moving to Ohio, the first test of Mitchell's resolve came in 1848 in Ross County. A slave from Maryland had escaped the clutches of his owner and established residence for several years in Ross and became an active member of the local Methodist church. He and his family felt protected in a free state and among residents who wished him no harm. However, to the shock and surprise of many, the minister of the church reported him, it was assumed, for the $100 reward that had been offered for the man.[167]

One day while working, three slave catchers surprised him, put a rope around his neck and dragged him outside the town limits quickly. The residents of color received word rapidly that one of their own had been captured. As word continued to spread, two hundred assembled and began to pursue the slave catchers. About three miles outside of town, the slave, with one end of the rope around his neck and the other end around the neck of a horse, and his captors saw the posse riding at top speed toward them. The slave catchers, realizing that their safety was in jeopardy, cut the rope loose from the horse and rode as hard as possible away from the clutches of their pursuers. The slave, a captive no longer, was taken back into town on the shoulders of his liberators.[168]

The busiest phase of Mitchell's Underground Railroad activity happened while he was living in Washington Courthouse, Ohio. One contributor to his activity was a former slave turned conductor, John Mason. During one nineteen-month period, Mitchell credited Mason with bringing 265 escaped slaves to his home. Mason alleged that he aided the escape of over 1,300 slaves himself.[169]

John Mason was eventually captured, sold and returned to bondage in New Orleans. However, he did not go quietly. In the struggle to take him, both of his arms were broken. Sticking his chest out he pleaded, "Put a ball in that! I don't wish to live any longer." Finally, following almost a year and a half, Mason informed Mitchell that he was in Hamilton, Canada West.[170]

Mitchell, like the other men and women who aided fugitive slaves, was doing so in defiance of the Fugitive Slave Law of 1850. In his opinion, though, the law only cemented the determination of those opposed to slavery to double their efforts to render it moot, saying, "It was a strange oversight on the part of the conservators of slavery, when they passed the Fugitive Bill (for law it is not)."[171] Mitchell's resolve was to see that the act's intended mission—to return the slave to his master and punish those who aided his escape—resulted instead in spurring abolitionists to even more resolute actions.

All of Mitchell's labors made him a target of the slaveholders and the slave catchers, however. In one instance, his house was surrounded by men who knew that he and his wife were hiding a fugitive and insisted that Mitchell let them come in and take the slave. Rather than panicking though, Mitchell was just as insistent that the slave catchers secure a warrant to enter his house. While they were gone, Mrs. Mitchell dressed the slave like a woman and spirited him to a safe house before the slave catchers could return with the warrant.[172]

Like his peers, the numbers of slaves whom Mitchell helped escape the bonds that held them to slavery are incalculable. Most of them were aided in their flight by seeing that they began a new life in Canada, away from the reach of the laws of the United States. It is not surprising then that William Mitchell moved to Canada in 1855 and worked for the American Baptist Free Mission Society. While there, he wrote his book *The Underground Railroad, From Slavery to Freedom*, which was published in 1860, just before the calamity of America's Civil War. Some of the profits from each book sold were donated to the mission house he founded in Toronto, Canada.[173]

Chapter 8

THE HEROINE OF EDENTON, HARRIET JACOBS

P erhaps no slave escape from North Carolina was more dramatic than that of Harriet Jacobs. Breathing free air, and with time for reflection, Harriet Jacobs, using the pseudonym "Linda Brent," published an account of her life, including a long and arduous flight that finally landed her in Philadelphia. The title of her narrative, which was first published in 1861, is called *Incidents in the Life of A Slave Girl*. It is a tale of anguish, courage and determination inspired by an unquenched longing for liberty, for herself and for her children.

For a while, beginning in 1722, Edenton, where Jacobs's story has its origins, served as North Carolina's British colonial capital. Although New Bern was selected in 1766 to be a more permanent seat of government, Edenton remained a bustling port. That was especially true during the years leading up to America's War of Independence, from about 1771 to 1776. During that five-year period, 828 ships came into and out of the town's port.[174]

Although the town did not remain as prosperous following the American Revolution, its proximity to the Dismal Swamp, on the border of North Carolina and Virginia, presented opportunities for fugitive slaves. Numerous flights for freedom were made out of Edenton and neighboring ports by runaways who initially sometimes hid in the Dismal before safe passage could be secured.

Ordinarily, slaves were field hands, skilled craftsmen or house servants. The life of a field hand was day after day, hour after hour of backbreaking labor. They toiled year round. When it wasn't planting season, it was time to

Harriet Jacobs, escaped slave, circa 1894. *Wikimedia.*

harvest; when it wasn't time to harvest, fields needed to be prepped. The life of a field hand was an entire existence of working in the scorching summer heat or the frozen temperatures of winter, which even in North Carolina can often be numbing.

The skilled laborers were carpenters, coopers and engineers, among others. These types of jobs were extremely valuable to a slave because they frequently offered freedoms that did not come with a field hand's existence. A skilled slave could work on neighboring farms or even in a nearby town or city. Their owner would literally rent them out, which put cash in the hands of the master but, more importantly, put cash in the hands of the bondsman. This was money that slaves regularly saved in order to purchase their freedom, if the master was of a mind to allow it.

Perhaps the most prized assignments were those of house servants. These jobs included maid, seamstress, butler, cook and body servant. They were coveted positions because they weren't constantly breathing the hot, dry dust of summer or suffering the bitter bite of winter, like their slave brethren in the fields. The lives of house servants were, as much as the life of a slave allowed, clean and comfortable jobs. It was as a house servant that Harriet toiled and suffered the indignities of sexual advances from her dreaded nemesis, Dr. James Norcom. Harriet referred to Dr. Norcom in *Incidents of a Slave Girl*, as "Dr. Flint."

Harriet did not use her real name nor the actual names of the others in her account in order to protect her family, individuals who aided her escape and herself. Because of her use of camouflaged names, many critics accused the editor, Lydia Maria Child, of fabricating the work herself, until Jean Fagan Yellin proved conclusively in the 1980s that the work was penned by Jacobs.[175]

Professor Yellin identified the characters referenced in *Incidents* and their real-life names. Of course, Harriet was "Linda," and Dr. Norcom was "Dr. Flint" in her narrative. Other important people in the account of her life were Mary Matilda Horniblow Norcom, Dr. Norcom's bitter and jealous wife, as "Mrs. Flint"; Harriet's grandmother, Molly Horniblow, as "Aunt Martha"; her little brother, John, as "William"; Harriet's white lover, Samuel Treadwell Sawyer as "Mr. Sands"; and the rector of St. Paul's Episcopal Church, Reverend Dr. Avery, as "Reverend Dr. Pike," as well as others.[176]

Harriet Jacob's tale of her life as a slave begins, with her admission, "I was born a slave; but I never knew it till six years of happy childhood had passed away." At that tender age, her mother died. It was only then, as she heard the talk around her, that she came to the realization that she was property.[177]

Harriet explains in her narrative that her father was a highly sought-after carpenter. He was so good at his trade that he was quite often requested when a construction project was underway that required special talents.

Dr. James Norcom, tormentor of Harriet Jacobs. *Courtesy of the State Archives of North Carolina.*

As a result, his arrangements with his mistress were uncommon to the degree that he was able to save money in the hopes that one day he would be permitted to purchase his children. For the sum of $200 a year, paid to his mistress, he was allowed to "manage his own affairs" while living in a secure and happy home with his family.[178]

Jacobs's grandmother Molly was the daughter of a planter in South Carolina. During the American Revolution, her father and master died. In his will, he freed Molly's mother, as well as her children. Money and passage to St. Augustine, Florida, were provided, where relatives lived. Tragically, they were captured during their trip and sold back into slavery, each going to a different owner.

Molly was purchased by the keeper of a hotel in Edenton, where her childhood was a hard one. However, she turned out to be such a bright and dedicated servant that her master and mistress both realized they had an exceptional piece of property. Her reputation as a cook, particularly for her crackers, advanced to the point that her services were constantly requested. As a result, Molly asked her mistress for permission to bake her famous crackers at night after all of her other obligations were completed. Her request was granted, as long as she used the profits to clothe herself and her children.[179]

So well loved was Molly that her mistress promised that, upon her death, she would be freed. The promise was indeed kept, but Molly's mistress was the sister of the man who would become the torturer of Harriet years later, Dr. Norcom. He was in charge of settling his sister's estate and told Molly that rather than being freed, she would need to be sold. When the day arrived for the fifty-year-old slave to be sold, many of the town's residents were upset that she was suffering the indignity and refused to place a bid for her. Finally, an elderly woman, the sister of Molly's deceased mistress, purchased her for fifty dollars, whereupon the slave was granted her freedom.[180]

Harriet's grandmother had, of course, hoped to one day purchase the freedom of her children. That was something that never happened, so Harriet's mother was in bondage when she died. She had been such a devoted servant that her mistress promised to care for Harriet and her brother following their mother's death. As long as the lady was alive, she was true to her word. Harriet, like her mother before her, served her mistress faithfully, and because she was treated well, the young girl was always happy to serve her.[181]

Unfortunately, around 1825, Harriet's mistress died, and the young twelve-year-old girl went to live with her grandmother for a week while she awaited her fate. She dared to hope that perhaps her mistress would allow her to go free in her will, but ultimately her hopes were dashed. Her mistress had willed her to the daughter of her sister, who was no more than five years old at the time. Harriet's life was about to sink to depths she could not even imagine. The father of her very young mistress was Dr. James Norcom.[182]

Over the next few years of the teenager's life, she experienced one horrible episode after another. About a year following the death of the mistress she had loved so well, her father died. On the day of her father's death, rather than being allowed to go to his house and mourn his passing with others, "I was ordered to go for flowers, that my mistress's house might be decorated for an evening party."[183] She was allowed to be present, however, when her father's body was laid to rest beside her mother the following day.

When Harriet was fourteen, Dr. Norcom began taking more interest in her and making advances toward her. She managed, through cunning, to avoid the kind of liaisons Norcom was suggesting, which only served to frustrate the old doctor. Sexual attention toward female slaves was not uncommon by their white masters in the slaveholding South, and often when their overtures were not returned in kind, the slaves suffered. That turned out to be the case with Harriet.

It was roughly around the same time that she fell deeply in love for the first time. She knew if Dr. Norcom learned about her love interest, he would do everything possible to "render me miserable." The man with whom Harriet had fallen in love was free, and he was more than agreeable to pay any reasonable price to the Norcoms so he and Harriet could marry. Norcom confronted her the day after he was informed of the proposed arrangement and demanded, "So you want to be married do you? And to a free nigger." At that, Harriet professed her love for the young man, which prompted Dr. Norcom to leap upon her and knock her to the floor.[184]

The treatment of Harriet at the hands of the Norcoms continued in a downward spiral as she matured. Knowing that the doctor was making advances toward the slave girl, Mrs. Norcom became bitter and jealous. She made Harriet remove a new pair of shoes that Harriet's grandmother had given her and forced the teenager to walk barefoot through the snow and cold of a February day on an errand. When Harriet went to bed hoarse that night, she thought she might be extremely sick the next morning or, perhaps, dead. However, "what was my grief on waking to find myself quite well!"[185]

Even in the face of knowing that Mrs. Norcom was well aware of his intentions toward Harriet, the doctor continued to pester and plot in order to force his slave to consent to his wishes. He began having a cabin built about four miles outside of town for the purpose of making Harriet live there and submit to his wishes. The young fifteen-year-old was desperate for a way out. It happened that, at the time the cabin was under construction, a young white gentleman began asking about Harriet. As the young man began showing interest in her, she was merely flattered at first, but then her feelings developed into something more.[186]

Harriet began an affair with the white man, whose name was Samuel Tredwell Sawyer. She referred to him as Mr. Sands in her narrative. Her affair resulted in her becoming pregnant, which sent Dr. Norcom into a rage. What was worse was her grandmother's reaction when she discovered Harriet's condition. One evening while Harriet was at her grandmother's house, she was trying to muster the courage to tell Molly she was pregnant when Mrs. Norcom stormed into the old black lady's house and wildly accused Harriet of carrying her husband's baby. Reacting to the moment, Molly told her granddaughter to leave her house and never return.[187]

In a short time, granddaughter and grandmother reconciled, and Harriet was able to explain the miserable treatment she had received at the hands of both the doctor and Mrs. Norcom. She was also able to enlighten Molly about how she had been desperate for some compassion and tenderness, which led her to accept the embrace of a white man. When Dr. Norcom found out the father of Harriet's child was a white man, however, it set him off into a jealous fury. It was all he could do to restrain himself and not hit her as he had done before.[188]

Samuel Sawyer had made offers to purchase Harriet, but Norcom vowed he would never sell her, which ruined any hopes she had of being rid of the old tyrant. When she gave birth to a boy, Dr. Norcom insisted upon caring for Harriet and her child. All the while, Harriet lived with her grandmother, just as she had done since Mrs. Norcom became suspicious of her and her husband. When the old doctor came to Molly's house, he resumed his suggestive innuendoes, sometimes thanked Harriet for adding to his slave count and threatened to sell her boy.[189]

Later, when Harriet told Dr. Norcom that she was again pregnant and that again it was Tredwell's child, he flew into such a rage that he took scissors and cut her hair extremely close to her scalp. She eventually gave birth to a girl, but regardless of the old miserable doctor's taunts and threats, it would have been hard for her to feel any real joy about bringing a girl into a world of slavery. As she wrote in her narrative, "Slavery is terrible for men; but it is far more terrible for women."[190]

As years passed, Harriet's life became increasingly unbearable. Dr. Norcom moved her out to his son's plantation house outside of town and away from her grandmother. He ordered her to move both of her children to the plantation as well, which was nothing more than an effort to keep her from escaping. She resolved to flee her slave condition rather than submit her children to the controlling grasp of James Norcom.

Knowing that Dr. Norcom intended to have her children delivered to the plantation the following day, Harriet stole out of the house that night in the rain and made good her escape back into town. There she went to her grandmother's house, where her children were. However, she did not dare let Molly know she was there. Rather, she tapped on the window of a lady who had lived in the house with her grandmother for several years and in whom she knew she could place her trust. Once inside, she crept into the room where her boy and girl slept, kissed each of them tenderly without waking them and left. From there, she trudged through the rain and darkness to the house of a friend and safe concealment.[191]

The next day, Dr. Norcom was at Molly's house demanding to know where Harriet was hiding. Just as Harriet had planned, the elderly lady could honestly claim she thought her granddaughter was at the plantation house. To make sure, her house was thoroughly searched. When no indications were found that hinted at Harriet's whereabouts, a complete search of all northbound ships in Edenton's docks was instigated, but with no sign of the fleeing twenty-one-year-old slave girl. Harriet had fled the licentious clutches of Dr. James Norcom, but it would be a very long time before she was truly free.[192]

As the search for her continued, she could never feel comfortable that she would not be discovered. One time she even suffered from the venomous effects of a snake bite when she had been compelled to hide in a thicket of bushes. Word of Harriet's place of hiding and her perilous condition was

Looking into the cell chamber of the Old Edenton Jail, as it appears today. *Image courtesy of Lee C. Miller.*

finally conveyed back to Molly. A white lady, the wife of a man who owned slaves but whom Molly trusted, agreed to conceal Harriet and see that she was nursed back to health.[193]

Part of Harriet's hope of running away was that Dr. Norcom might sell her young son and daughter. Mr. Sawyer, the father of the children, was also hoping the old doctor might agree to sell them, because it was his intention to buy them when the opportunity arose. Harriet, who was still hiding in town, was shocked and saddened when Norcom had her children thrown in jail, in order to force someone to reveal her whereabouts. As badly as she wanted to run to the aid of her offspring, she dared not. She would have been forced to reveal where she had been hiding, which would implicate the people who had been protecting her.[194]

Dr. Norcom became convinced that Harriet had made her way to New York. Therefore, he secured a loan from an influential lady in town so that he might go there and look for his slave. Unaware that he had just borrowed money from the lady who was presently hiding Harriet, he made a thorough but futile search for her.[195]

Upon his return to Edenton, Dr. Norcom was approached by a slave trader about purchasing Harriet's brother and children. Reluctant but desperately needing the money after his New York expenses, Norcom agreed to sell all three of the slaves. He had no way of knowing it at that moment, but he had been duped by Samuel Tredwell Sawyer, who had sent the slave trader to seek a deal with the old man. As soon as the trader had the rights to Harriet's brother, son and daughter, he sold them to Sawyer. A great show was made to make it appear as though the trader was taking them off to be bonded in another location. However, they were released, and the children were returned to Molly's house.[196]

Ultimately, Harriet left the security of her hiding place with her white, female benefactor. Under cover of darkness and escorted by a black man she called Peter in her book, the fugitive made her way by boat to Snaky Swamp. She hid there for a while before clandestinely concealing herself in the attic of a shed that had recently been added to her grandmother's house. It offered no ventilation and only the room that a hiding place nine feet long, seven feet wide and three feet high could give her. However, in spite of the discomforts of her living quarters, she could hear the noises and voices of her children.[197]

These cramped quarters were where Harriet remained for the next *seven* years—seven years of insects and their bites; of stifling, sweltering heat in the summertime; and the stinging, frostbitten cold of winters. Seven years of listening to Christmas celebrations in which she could not take part, and seven years in which she could not hold her children. Seven years of torturous agony, as her body wilted without the freedom to freely move about and exercise. However, during these years, Harriet and her grandmother Molly saw to it that Mr. Sawyer got their daughter to Brooklyn—and freedom, education and a chance. It was also during her confinement that Dr. Norcom became convinced through clever deception that Harriet was in New York, or Boston, never to return to his clutches.

Finally, the man Harriet refers to as Peter came to her and said that her best chance to escape to the North had arrived. At first, Molly was agreeable to the plan, but as the time grew closer, the old woman grew despondent and worried. For her sake, Harriet agreed not to go and arranged to have another female slave, whom she knew was in hiding nearby, go in her place. The very next evening, Harriet's friend was secured onboard a vessel. Yet the vessel did not leave port due to a headwind.[198]

Three days later, it was feared that a housemaid who could not be trusted had seen Harriet when she had climbed out of her nest to talk to her grandmother. The untrustworthy visitor had stopped by for some of Molly's famous crackers. At that point, the old lady knew there was no choice but for Harriet to make her run while the ship was still available. As luck would have it, however, the ship had finally caught a favorable wind and was underway downstream. Quickly, Peter caught a boat to the ship and persuaded the captain to wait until that evening.[199]

As the day passed, it became apparent that the housemaid had not seen Harriet, but she was determined, as was her grandmother, that she should finally make her run for the free states. She was resolute that she would see her son and reveal her secret before she departed. With a tearful goodbye to him, and a promise to get him to the North as soon as possible, she then, with a heavy heart, bid farewell to Molly, her dear grandmother. At the appointed hour, she stepped out into the street, where she joined up with Peter. They swiftly made their way to the wharf and caught a rowboat out to the awaiting vessel, where she was secreted below, along with her fleeing companion.[200]

After about ten days sailing, the ship approached Philadelphia and docked that evening. The captain had the two women wait until the next morning and disembark in the light of day to lessen suspicion. When dawn arrived the next morning, Harriet was on deck to watch the sky begin its morning glow for the first time as a free person. Her fellow traveler joined her as they stepped off of the vessel and into Philadelphia. Both of them wept.[201]

Later, Harriet was joined by both of her children. At one point, she had to run to New England from New York because of the threat of being caught by slave catchers, due to the 1850 Fugitive Slave Law. Her life had been at times suffocating, even horrid, and at other times full and heartwarming.

Before her death in March 1897, at the age of eighty-four, she wrote, lectured in the United States and Europe and suffered the indignation of northern discrimination. In England, she spoke to crowds of the curious and sympathetic. She accomplished things in her life that many women of the nineteenth century, regardless of color, only dreamed of.

Perhaps her emotions concerning the writing of her narrative are summed up best in her final paragraph: "It has been painful to me in many ways, to recall the dreary years I passed in bondage. I would gladly forget them if I could. Yet the retrospection is not altogether without solace; for with those gloomy recollections come tender memories of my good old grandmother, like light, fleecy clouds floating over a dark and troubled sea."[202]

Chapter 9

RUNAWAYS DURING THE CIVIL WAR

William H. Siebert, in his 1898 book, *The Underground Railroad: From Slavery to Freedom*, points out, "Underground operations practically ceased with the beginning of the Civil War."[203] Siebert's work looks almost exclusively at Northern states, so his conclusion means that with the commencement of the war, slaves in the South were now at the mercy of their owners or, if they tried to escape, their own wits and various networks of slaves and freed blacks with occasional assistance from sympathetic whites. For the first year of the war, Southern victories were the news of the day, and there was no doubt many a day of fear and trepidation among the slave communities and shanties, wondering what would happen should the South win.

However, Seibert's conclusion ignores one facet of the Underground Railroad that has been overlooked: whites used it, too. Union sympathizers, Quakers who fled persecution, Union soldiers who had been captured and were on their way to Salisbury to imprisonment but had escaped and others used the Underground Railroad to escape the South.[204] Along with this, Confederate soldiers used the Underground Railroad as a means of escape from enlistment and later conscription, the forcing of deserters back into the Confederate ranks. Three stories illustrate this peculiar twist in Underground Railroad lore.

First, as the war started Southern-born captains of United States Navy ships were required to swear oaths of loyalty to the Union. James I. Waddell, anticipating the escalating tension, hoped that war would not ensue but privately noted that he would serve in the South if forced to choose. In November 1861, Waddell sent in his resignation as a U.S. Navy ship captain on the USS *John Adams*. While the request was being considered, he continued to fulfill his duties. Landing in New York City, he was forced to take an oath of loyalty if he wished to return to his home and wife in Annapolis, where he had taught at the Naval Academy, which he did under protest. In January 1862, Waddell was dismissed from the military. Still, he was a wanted man. In this instance, he had to escape *to* the Confederacy. He privately contacted some underground smugglers who worked the border states and, along with other escapees, fled to the South, where he quickly signed up for a commission as a lieutenant in the Confederate States navy.[205]

From 1861 into 1862 in the eastern part of Tennessee, pro-Union George Kirk would slip over to the western mountain regions of North Carolina and bring back Confederate draft dodgers and deserters on an underground railroad. Kirk eventually was drafted into service for the Union, where he initially served as captain of the Fifth East Tennessee Cavalry. By 1863, he was given command of a new unit, the Second Regiment North Carolina Mounted Infantry, United States. By 1864, he was in charge of the Third Regiment North Carolina Mounted Infantry, United States. Ironically, some of the Confederate deserters and runaway slaves who fled for safety on his underground railroad later joined his unit to fight against Confederate forces in Western North Carolina.[206] Tennessee was a slave state, and slaves who joined Kirk's forces certainly did not return from the North to the South risking capture. Most likely they were in hiding in safe communities in the mountains. How else would Kirk have known of them?

According to Eric J. Richardson, Quakers in the Piedmont of North Carolina—more specifically from the area of Snow Camp and Cane Creek Quaker Meeting to Greensboro—who originally used the Underground Railroad to move slaves to the North began hiding and aiding Confederate deserters, many of whom were also raiding, pillaging and terrorizing the area. As troops from the Fifty-second North Carolina Regiment and the Seventh North Carolina State Troops moved into the region, they conducted interviews with local women who, tired of the havoc being wreaked upon their families, disclosed the locations of probable stops on the Underground Railroad. In one instance, Confederate privates Mullen and Oberman created a ruse to find out how an elderly white man and a free black man were hiding the deserters. It is not known how many deserters were transported to freedom by local Quakers and other sympathizers.[207]

Coastal slaves often served as workers on the docks, piloted small boats in the inlets or plied their trades in various occupations such as coopers (barrel makers), sawyers and millers, as well as labored in the tar and pitch industry. Since all of these involved some contact either directly or indirectly with the shipping industry, slaves were exposed to ideas and the means of freedom from the outside world. Thus, "many slaves became infused with the ideas of freedom in the larger world introduced by black seamen who frequented the ports," as Judkin Browning notes.[208] The Civil War offered yet another manner of escape for bondsmen and bondswomen.

In 1861, Northern forces began their assault on the Outer Banks of North Carolina. Today known as the "Graveyard of the Atlantic," this area of dangerous shoals and ever-shifting islands and inlets would soon be recognized as key to infiltrating North Carolina, one-third of whose residents were Union sympathizers. A Union blockade of Southern ports was immediately put into action after Fort Sumter was bombarded and Southern states seceded from the Union. Southern blockade runners often broke through to bring supplies to rebel ports. In the summer of 1861, one hundred blockade runners successfully navigated the shoals and dodged the Union ships to unload their cargoes on Confederate soil.

As North Carolina built a string of makeshift forts along the Outer Banks, Union leaders formed a plan to attack and invade the coast. Soon the fort at Cape Hatteras was taken, and Confederates retreated to Roanoke Island. But fears were strong that the rebels would counterattack, even though evidence of such an attack was lacking.

With the capture of coastal forts, local slaves now had an even greater excuse to escape. Looking to the Union troops as saviors, slaves made plans to flee their coastal and inland plantations for the coast. As they made their way to the Union encampments, they were questioned by the troops, who were looking for information regarding Confederate troops' placements and movements and armaments. Not all slaves brought reliable information. No doubt misled by worried masters, they often provided false or highly misleading information to the Union interrogators. Union colonel Rush Hawkins, on September 21, 1861, heard news that worried him greatly as he interviewed runaway slaves that day. The former slaves of Samuel Jarvis on Roanoke Island warned of rebel forces numbering over eight thousand infantry who were preparing to attack Hatteras with the intent of hanging all the Union soldiers.[209] As it turned out, not only was this was a huge exaggeration, but it was also entirely false.

By early 1862, what was called the Burnside Expedition was put into action. Union general Ambrose E. Burnside would lead the army component of a strike on the Island of Roanoke. From there, he would then move south and west to capture the port towns of New Bern, Beaufort and Fort Macon, as well as move north to the Albemarle and Chesapeake Canal. As the Confederates embarked to reinforce Roanoke Island, the Federals began staging at Hatteras for the assault. On February 5, the 7,500 Northern soldiers loaded in the ships in Pamlico Sound and headed north. They paused for the night just south of Roanoke Island. General Burnside questioned a young fugitive slave, Thomas Robinson, about the island. Where was the best place to land? Robinson directed him to Ashby's Harbor, a few miles up on the west side of the island. As it turned out, the runaway slave's information was very useful. The ill-trained, poorly clad, disorganized, mostly illiterate and otherwise hapless Confederates, thinking that the Union forces would land on the north side of the island, had beefed up their reinforcements there. As Union and Confederate ships traded fire, Union soldiers unloaded safely at Ashby's Harbor on February 7. On February 8, an assault toward the northern Confederate forts on the island was begun, and by day's end the Battle of Roanoke Island was over: it was now in the hands of the Union.

That evening, the Union troops celebrated their victory by slaughtering livestock on the island and feeding themselves, the prisoners of war and some of the locals. Blacks, who just hours before were mere chattel, joined in the celebration as well. They rushed to show the Union troops where whites had hidden stores of food.[210]

Once word got out to the inland plantations that Union forces had taken Roanoke Island, it was now east, not north, that many North Carolina slaves fled.

Burnside then set his sights on New Bern, and on March 14, his troops captured the city. Many newly freed slaves participated with Union troops in looting but not for long, resulting in little damage. Still, the once-prosperous city was desolate except for wandering poor blacks and curious Northern soldiers. Burnside soon put many former bondsmen to work with wages of eight dollars a month, plus clothing and food. By the end of April, Fort Macon had also fallen, leaving the port town of Beaufort open for capture. If storeowners did not swear allegiance to the Union, their businesses and homes were taken from them. Former slaves, whom Beaufort residents naively thought were loyal to their masters and thus the South, often looted these buildings that were abandoned by Confederate loyalists.[211]

All was not safe for some slaves and free blacks, however. Edward Stanly was made governor of North Carolina in 1862, and he governed from the palace in New Bern. He believed in the Union goals of reuniting the states, but he also believed that slavery should remain intact. In fact, this is what many Union officials desired: the union of the states while retaining their own particular institutions, including slavery. Thus, Stanly decreed that any slaves who escaped to the Union were fugitives and were to be returned to their masters. Families who lost slaves were given permission to search for them, and any found were to return to their masters. In a defiant move, some Union troops sought out the now re-enslaved blacks and kidnapped them away from their owners at gunpoint. Stanly could not stop the efforts of these renegade Union troops, even though General Burnside had warned his troops to desist from such tactics. Caught in the middle were innocent slaves who could literally be free one day, a slave the next and free after that unless they were scurried away to a secret place by their masters, never to be heard from again.[212]

One daring and brave slave escape from Civil War Wilmington took place in the evening and early morning hours of September 21 to 22. From the Orange Street Landing, eight slaves stole away in a rowboat. One of the men in the small craft was William B. Gould, born in Wilmington on November 18, 1837, who was not only a skilled plasterer and brick mason but also literate. Taking the boat was only the beginning of a twenty-eight-nautical-mile journey that took them past Fort Caswell, one of the few remaining Confederate strongholds on the Southern coast, and finally out into the Atlantic, where they were seen by two ships of the Union's North Atlantic Blockading Squadron.[213]

William Gould would ultimately serve in the same United States Navy that rescued him and his seven fellow weary runaways that morning of September 22. While he served in the navy from 1862 to 1865, he kept a diary that became the basis of the book, published in 2002, *Diary of a Contraband: The Civil War Passage of a Black Sailor.* The book was put together by Gould's great-grandson William B. Gould IV.

However, if Gould's experience that fateful morning was not enough, sixteen additional slaves grabbed small boats that morning of September 22 as well. In all, twenty-two men took charge of their lives and chanced swift, sure and cruel punishment if caught to become free. After the war, it appears that at least one of Gould's fellow conspirators of that morning returned to North Carolina.

Following the cessation of hostilities, William Gould moved to Dedham, Massachusetts, in 1871. There, he lived out his life as a father, husband, contractor and active member of the Episcopal Church of the Good Shepherd. Both he and his wife were baptized and confirmed into the Episcopal Church in 1788 and 1789, respectively.[214]

One of the men who made his way to freedom in September 1862 was George Price. Price would eventually represent New Hanover County in the North Carolina House of Representatives from 1869 to 1870. Price also served in the North Carolina Senate from 1870 to 1872 and was said to be an outstanding orator.[215] Following the war, Reconstruction Wilmington became a Republican fortress, and newly freed blacks flocked to that political party.

Except for Wilmington, the coast of North Carolina was in the hands of the Union. Now plans were drawn for attacks on the inland cities of Goldsboro and Raleigh. But these plans were thwarted because of Confederate victories in Virginia that led to Burnside being called back to that arena. In his absence, Union general John G. Foster began fortifying New Bern with considerable earthworks and forts. Escaped slaves assisted the Union soldiers who built these fortifications.[216]

It is here that we see a shift in slave "escapes." Foster led a force of five thousand men toward Tarboro on October 31. Deserted small towns were looted, plundered and burned. While the main objective of capturing Confederate troops was not realized, liberating slaves, by capturing them, was. In 1863, Confederate forces began counterattacks, but in mid-July, more Union raids were conducted as well, and many "contrabands" were captured and brought back to New Bern.

For the rest of the year, life was quiet in eastern North Carolina. As more and more slaves fled east, male slaves would soon form Union regiments, which would be utilized in raids that secured the freedom of more North Carolina slaves.

Confederate forces tried to retake New Bern but failed. They were more successful in their recapture of the town of Plymouth, an important supply station for Union troops. Nearly three thousand soldiers were garrisoned there, as well as cavalry and artillery units and two companies of former Confederates who now fought for the Union side (these "traitors" were known as buffaloes). Also, there were around eighty black recruits and one thousand contrabands. The lives of the buffaloes, the black soldiers and contrabands were mostly at risk should the rebels achieve victory because Confederate policy now was that any buffalo captured would be hung for treason, any black soldiers caught were to be shot on the spot and any slaves captured were re-enslaved. The Confederates won, and the buffaloes, black soldiers and former slaves fled for the nearby swamps. Their goal was to head east toward Union strongholds. The Confederates, three companies of cavalry and one infantry strong, raced to the swamps and hunted down and killed nearly all blacks who fled Plymouth. Estimates are that nearly six hundred blacks and buffaloes were killed in one day. Women and children who were captured were put back into slavery. Freedom for these ex-slaves was short-lived.[217]

After the capture of coastal ports, slaves flocked to these new sanctuaries. Refugee camps were constructed in Beaufort, Hatteras, New Bern, Plymouth, Roanoke Island and Washington. Over ten thousand former slaves were living in these areas by June 1862. In January 1864, the number reached over seventeen thousand. Two of these camps have received extensive attention from scholars: the Freedman's Colony on Roanoke Island and James City, near New Bern.[218]

Once Roanoke Island was captured from the Confederates in February 1862, slaves passed the word throughout the coastal areas that freedom was close by. Over 200 slaves worked at the Confederate camps before they were captured. Interestingly, many of these slaves, once offered their freedom by the Northern troops, refused. Instead they wanted to risk their freedom and safety by going back to the mainland and finding their families in order to bring them back to the island. Slaves from Elizabeth City, Plymouth and Edenton made their way to the island. Slaves also hid in the woods, waiting for the chance to safely scurry to the island and freedom. Slaves who had hid in the Dismal Swamp, one since 1855, found a new life on Roanoke Island. In just two months, the population was about 250 freedmen and women. By 1864, nearly 3,000 ex-slaves were living in the colony.[219]

In *James City: A Black Community in North Carolina 1863–1900*, Joe A. Mobley briefly recounts the last days' exodus of slaves from their farms and masters to freedom in the camps of Union soldiers.[220] Whispers through the grapevine that began in Roanoke Island and spread westward to the North Carolina mainland told of Yankee troops coming. When General Ambrose E. Burnside marched to New Bern in the spring of 1862, slaves left their tools in the fields, grabbed what meager belongings they could and fled to freedom. The migration would soon lead to several camps and eventually cities such as James City.

Any slaves who slipped over to the Federal camps were considered contraband of war and were not released to their former owners. When New Bern was captured on March 14, slaves greeted their "saviors." As word spread, slaves sought the safety of the woods or swamps during the days and then made for the federal camps in New Bern, Washington, Elizabeth City and other places by night. Some arrived safely in small boats and rafts. As for others, those who could swim did so across rivers.

Some slaves did not have to resort to hiding. When Union troops went out on patrols to the distant sites of Goldsboro, Kinston and Tarboro, some slaves would find them and then receive a military escort back to their new homes. As the numbers of freed slaves grew, four areas became their havens: New Bern, Roanoke Island, Washington and Beaufort. One Union soldier observed, "The freed people came into my yard from neighboring plantations, sometimes as many as one hundred at a time, leaving with joy their plows in the fields, and their old homes, to follow our soldiers when returning from their frequent raids; the women carrying their pickanannies and the men huge bundles of bedding and clothing occasionally with a cart or old wagon, with a mule drawing their household stuff."[221]

The ex-slaves went right to work, building fortifications and bridges, handling ordnance, loading and unloading ships. Some even served as spies and risked their lives and freedom to provide information for the Yankee troops. Most worked for one meal a day and a small salary. Some found work in the homes and businesses of free blacks in New Bern. A few even became rich! Others joined the Union forces to fight against the very ones who once enslaved them.

But Northern attitudes toward the blacks were not always altruistic. Teachers and missionaries from the North were often guilty of paternalism. They, like their Southern counterparts, believed that slaves were inferior to the white race and thus needed constant supervision. What the Northern benevolent folks found was a resilient and headstrong group of blacks who knew exactly what kind of education they needed to survive in the South. As whites and blacks negotiated and reimagined this new freedom, eventually an understanding was reached and progress was made that was more suited to the needs of the former slaves than to the preconceived notions of Northern societies.[222]

Some former slaves outwitted their benevolent friends by acting the very part of the ignorant and weak souls in order to take advantage of Northern generosity. Playing out the condescending and paternalistic stereotypes, blacks received many rewards in the form of shoes, clothing, food and shelter, while the Northern benevolent administrators and missionaries were none the wiser.[223]

Likewise, not all of the Northern troops treated the former slaves respectfully. Some blamed them for the war itself; others abused them and made fun of them. It did not help that some of the former slaves refused to do any work or mutinied. But overall, the former bondsmen and women were appreciative of their liberators and glad of their often sparse and primitive conditions. And as it became more evident that the South would lose the war, more blacks fled to the coastal areas for freedom. As the numbers soared, freedmen's camps emerged. Some of these camps were attacked by advancing Confederate troops, and blacks were killed or forced to flee for their lives once more. Other camps flourished, and even fed poor whites, who were also victims of the pillaging and ravages of the war.

WHERE TO GO

I f the above narrative has whetted your appetite to explore the slave escapes and Underground Railroad in North Carolina, then the following information will be helpful.

On the National Park Service Website for the Underground Railroad there are twelve "sites" in eastern North Carolina that are worth investigating further. (The information from the site map "windows" is copied below.)

On the Roanoke River, just above Roanoke Rapids:
The Roanoke River represents both fishing and tobacco industries on the river, freedom seekers attempting several escapes, stealing and manning their owner's vessels, running to childhood plantations, and visiting relatives. The common denominators in the majority of the escapes on the Roanoke, Neuse, and Pasquotank rivers is that enslaved people needed and wanted to be with their families, wanted freedom, and attempted repeated escapes regardless of the consequences.

Just south and to the east of Roanoke Rapids is another location, the old town of Halifax:
The antebellum-era town of Halifax, NC, was a major destination for freedom seekers. Although the Roanoke River was clearly an UGRR waterway route, the river is not the only reason for escape activity to and from Halifax. Halifax had one of the largest free Black communities in North Carolina, had a large skilled class of enslaved artisans, and existed

in close proximity to an actively, abolitionist Quaker population. Based on the number of runaway slave ads indicating the town of Halifax as a final destination, one can conclude that Halifax provided a safe refuge for freedom seekers. Approximately 59 runaway slave advertisements from 1791 to 1840 were posted for 70 freedom seekers running to the town of Halifax. Slave owners specified in the runaway ads that slaves ran to the town of Halifax for several reasons, as listed: having a trade, being known in Halifax; attempting to pass as free; visiting a friend or relative; being hidden by someone in Halifax; having been caught once before in Halifax; etc. The UGRR in Halifax clearly represents the confluence of many communities, slave and free, along with the geographic identifiers of Halifax's border river, the Roanoke.

On Road 561, just southwest of rich square is an old cemetery:
This house burned in 1975, Henry and Dorothy Copeland's burial sites are being nominated. This cemetery site itself is significant as it contains the graves of other Quakers who were said to be associated with the UGRR. All were members of Rich Square Monthly Meeting in Rich Square, NC. On Henry Copeland's stone are the words: "The path of the Just is as the shining Light that shineth more and more unto the perfect day." And on his wife, Dorothy's stone: "She hath done all she could."

In Edenton:
The Edenton, NC waterfront served as a departure point for the Maritime Underground Railroad. This network was developed in North Carolina by African-American watermen who were able to arrange passage to northern states for fugitive slaves through their knowledge and expertise in maritime activities. One well-documented example is Harriet Jacob's account of her 1842 escape from Edenton by ship. Her escape was arranged by a waterman named Peter. Jacobs describes in "Incidents in the Life of a Slave Girl, Written by Herself," the arrangements Peter made in advance, how plans to transport her to a waiting ship were carried out, her fear of being found out, and her thankfulness when disembarking in Philadelphia that her friend Peter had correctly judged the ship captain's character. This example is not only of one individual's escape to freedom, but also of the network that existed making that escape possible. Jacobs' autobiograhpy [*sic*] was published in 1861 with names and places changed. In 1987, the actual names of characters were authenticated and found to have been residents of Edenton, NC.

Southwest of Elizabeth City:
The Pasquotank River runs between Pasquotank and Camden Counties in northeast North Carolina. The river flows past Elizabeth City to the Albemarle Sound. The Albemarle Sound runs into the Atlantic Ocean. The Great Dismal Swamp Canal, completed in 1805, connects the Cheaspeake [sic] Bay in Virginia via the Elizabeth River and the Albermarle Sound via the Pasquotank River. During the antebellum period in northeast North Carolina, rivers, canals, and sounds were not only essential for commerce and shipping, but played an important role in assisting enslaved African Americans to freedom via vessels and ships on route to northern states, Canada, and the Caribbean.

At the Virginia/North Carolina Border in the Great Dismal Swamp:
This huge area is jointly owned. US Fish and Wildlife manages over 111,000 acres stretching from Suffolk and Chesapeake, VA, to Camden, Pasqotan, and Gates Counties, NC as the Great Dismal Swamp National Wildlife Refuge. The State of NC manages 14,700 acres as Great Dismal Swamp State Park. US Army Corps of Engineers manages Dismal Swamp Canal, along Rte. 17 in VA and NC. NC DOT runs the Dismal Swamp Canal Welcome Center, and Elizabeth City State University manages 600 acres. There are also private owners. The application is jointly sponsored by the 4 mentioned owners.

In Manteo are three sites:
Between 1862 and 1867, approximately 3,000 slaves sought the protection of the Union army. In May 1863, they established a permanent colony. Slaves, who perished from wounds, illnesses, and diseases, were buried in mass graves within the grounds now designated as Memorial Garden, as were many freedmen who went on to establish residency on Roanoke Island.

In August of 1861, Union forces defeated Confederate batteries at Hatteras Inlet and at Forts Clark and Hatteras. Word of this victory spread quickly and prompted large numbers of enslaved people to escape from the mainland and Roanoke Island to freedom on Hatteras Island. Responsibility for sheltering and feeding these former enslaved people fell on the Union forces. Hotel De'Afrique was part of that provision. Hundreds of runaways arrived and in exchange for unloading supply vessels received food and housing. Many of these freedom seekers were able to provide strategic information regarding Confederate positions. This information led to Union victories. Hotel De'Afrique was the first contraband camp to be established by the military in North Carolina, therefore providing the first safe haven for freedom seekers in the state. There were two sites for Hotel De'Afrique on Forts Clark and Hatteras. They have both since disappeared due to erosion and flooding. A monument was established to tell the story in April 2012. The Hotel De'Afrique Monument is located at Cape Hatteras National Seashore, a national park service site in Hatteras, North Carolina.

Fort Raleigh National Historic Site is located on Roanoke Island, North Carolina. In 1862, under the command of General Ambrose E. Burnside, Union forces took control of the Outer Banks with the battle of Roanoke Island, and used the captured land to provide protection and freedom for runaways. Roanoke Island soon became known as a place of refuge for those who sought protection of the Union Army. Although some freedom seekers continued their journey northward, many of the refugees remained on the island. The number of "contraband" grew to exceed available housing, and to remedy this siutation [*sic*] General John G. Foster appointed Reverend Horace James, an army chaplain from Massachusetts, to establish a camp for runaways. This camp—Freedmen's Colony of Roanoke Island—came to serve as a model for future colonies, such as the one established in New Bern, North Carolina.

Washington, NC:

Some Somerset Place freedom seekers chose suicide over enslavement, others attempted murder, and still others expressed system hostility and frustration by burning their owner's property to the ground. Nineteen people ran away for a total of twenty-eight times with most suffering a myriad of sadly predictable retaliatory consequences: recapture, brutal punishment or being sold. When their bondage ended in 1865, however, 221 ex-slaves embraced all of freedom's promises by walking away foreever [*sic*] from everything their hands had created at Somerset Place. For them finally, there was, "no such thing to the next best thing to freedom."

New Bern/Neuse River:

Enslaved African Americans escaping to visit relatives on another plantation or in another town was most important, and one of the main reasons for escape. The significance of the family unit and the concept of community are dominant in the ads for the Neuse River and its contributing tributaries, and a majority of these runaway ads posted are for family members visiting each other, hiding each other until flight could safely continue, running to another plantation to take a loved one along for the attempted escape, "lying-out" near the edge of their plantation or another plantation for extended periods of time, and enslaved and free black people hiding freedom seekers on their plantations.

Wilmington, Orange Street Landing:

One of the slaves, William Benjamin Gould, kept the only known Civil War diary of a black soldier who was former slave. His great-grandson, Stanford University professor William B. Gould IV, has published *Diary of a Contraband: The Civil War Passage of a Black Sailor.*

There are two other major locations for the Underground Railroad in North Carolina. In Greensboro on the campus of Guilford College one can learn more about the Quakers and their role in the Underground Railroad. Visit the Hege Library and the fine collection of documents there and receive information about other places in the vicinity that pertain to the Underground Railroad.

In the small community of Snow Camp, just south of Burlington, are several sites important for the Underground Railroad. At the corner of Chapel Hill–Greensboro Highway and Sylvan School Road is Cane Creek Quaker Meeting. Across the road from the Meeting is Yesterday's Grill and behind that is a small shed that used to be the kitchen for the Thomas Dixon family. The old farm house has long since been destroyed but family lore indicates that runaways were hidden in a small potato cellar underneath the floor boards in the separate kitchen. Interestingly, Harriet Jacobs hid in a similar potato cellar. About a mile south on Sylvan Road was the location for Freedom's Hill Wesleyan Church. Runaways were hidden beneath the church or in a nearby abandoned home site or in a nearby hollow log. Freedom's Hill Wesleyan Church has been moved to Southern Wesleyan University in Central, South Carolina.

NOTES

Introduction

1. Genovese, *Roll Jordan, Roll*, 656.
2. "Slavery as We've Heard It," digital collection, Greensboro Historical Museum: http://archives.greensborohistory.org/digital/slavery.
3. Della Rose, *Daily Herald*, April 4, 2013, and updated April 8, 2013, http://www.rrdailyherald.com/news/underground-railroad-debate-in-weldon/article_56d13b32-9d3e-11e2-b7fa-0019bb2963f4.html
4. http://www.rrspin.com/roanoke-rapids-weldon-halifax-county-nc-news/item/6391-underground-railroad-lecture-series-topic.html.
5. Weeks, *Southern Quakers and Slavery*; Crow, Escott and Hatley, *African Americans in North Carolina*; Genovese, *Roll, Jordan, Roll*; Powell, *North Carolina Through Four Centuries*; Ready, *Tarheel State*; Cecelski, *Waterman's Song*.
6. Blockson, "Underground Railroad," 3–39.
7. Seibert, *The Underground Railroad, From Slavery to Freedom*, 58.
8. Beal, *Southern Friend*, 2:24.
9. See the video "Was Mendenhall Plantation an Underground Railroad Station" at http://library.guilford.edu/c.php?g=142981&p=.
10. Tobin and Dobard, Hidden in Plain View. For the critique see http://historiccamdencounty.com/ccnews11_doc_01a.shtml. Interestingly, the family of one of Tim's students has one of these quilts from that time.
11. The New Century Hymnal (Cleveland: The Pilgrim Press, 1995), hymn 369; Clinton, Harriet Tubman; Blockson, "Underground Railroad," 39.

12. Retrieved from http://library.guilford.edu/c.php?g=142981&p=934740; Thurman, Deep River.
13. Ready, *Tarheel State*, chapter 5.
14. Franklin, *Free Negro*, 41, 39, note 132.
15. Ready, *Tarheel State*, 81.
16. Gara, *Liberty Line*.
17. Coffin, *Life and Travels*, 36–40.
18. Ibid., 41.
19. Gara, *Liberty Line*, 144
20. Home Box Office, *Unchained Memories: Readings from the Slave Narratives* (Boston: Bulfinch Press, 2002), chapter 7.
21. Siebert, *Underground Railroad*, 50.
22. Sherburne, *Abolition and the Underground Railroad*.
23. Weeks, *Southern Quakers and Slavery*, 232–33.

Chapter 1

24. http://www.pbs.org/wgbh/aia/part4/4p2944.html.
25. http://www.nps.gov/nr/travel/underground/.
26. http://ncpedia.org/underground-railroad.
27. Gara, *Liberty Line*, 91.
28. Coffin, *Life and Travels*, 7.
29. Coffin, *Reminiscences*, 171–72.
30. See, for example, Calarco, *Search for the Underground Railroad*; VanHorne-Lane, *Safe Houses and the Underground Railroad*; Velsor, *Underground Railroad on Long Island*; Bordewich, *Bound for Canaan*.
31. Retrieved from http://www.nps.gov/nr/travel/underground/detailedroutes.htm.

Chapter 2

32. Franklin and Moss, *From Slavery to Freedom*, 57.
33. Chernow, *Washington*, 802.
34. Bassett, *Anti-Slavery Leaders*, 63, 64.
35. Franklin and Moss, *From Slavery to Freedom*, 149.
36. Bassett, *Anti-Slavery Leaders*, 10.
37. Middlekauff, *Glorious Cause*, 556.

38. Crow, *Black Experience in Revolutionary North Carolina*, 100.
39. Franklin and Moss, *From Slavery to Freedom*, 143.
40. McDougall, *Fugitive Slaves*, 7.
41. Franklin and Moss, *From Slavery to Freedom*, 81.
42. Ibid., 184.
43. Stashower, *Hour of Peril*, 27.
44. Franklin and Moss, *From Slavery to Freedom*, 184.
45. Allen, *Snow Camp*, 105.
46. Franklin and Moss, *From Slavery to Freedom*, 188.
47. Coffin, *Early Settlement of Friends*, 121, 177.
48. Ibid., 122.
49. Ibid., 123.
50. Ibid., 123–24.
51. Ibid., 126.
52. Ibid., 124.
53. Ibid., 125–26.
54. Ibid., 127–28.
55. Ibid., 144.
56. Ibid., 145.
57. Coffin, *Reminiscences of Levi Coffin*, 74.
58. Cecelski, *The Waterman's Song*, 124.
59. Ibid.; Boles, *Black Southerners*, 119.

Chapter 3

60. From the North Carolina Newspaper Digitization Project; http://cdm16062.contentdm.oclc.org/cdm/search/collection/p15016coll1/searchterm/runaway/field/all/mode/all/conn/and/order/nosort/cosuppress/1/page/3; Accessed 11/04/2014.
61. Crow, *The Black Experience*, 40.
62. Parker, *Running for Freedom*, 30.
63. Ibid.
64. Ibid., 30–31.
65. Crow, *The Black Experience*, 19.
66. From a Library of Congress website named, "America's Story from America's Library"; http://www.americaslibrary.gov/jb/colonial/jb_colonial_stono_2.html; Accessed 11/14/2014.
67. Parker, *Running for Freedom*, 32.

68. Crow, *Black Experience*, 22.

69. Parker, *Running for Freedom*, 38.

70. Franklin and Moss, *From Slavery to Freedom*, 125.

71. Monk, *Words We Live By*, 104.

72. Ibid., 107.

73. Ibid.

74. Crow, *Black Experience*, 42.

75. Parker, *Stealing a Little Freedom*, 753.

Chapter 4

76. Lefler, *North Carolina History*, 263.

77. Ibid., 263–64.

78. North Carolina Runaway Slave Advertisements, 1751–1840, University of North Carolina-Greensboro: http://libcdm1.uncg.edu/cdm/landingpage/collection/RAS. Information from this site was accessed multiple times so access dates have not been provided.

79. http://libcdm1.uncg.edu/cdm/singleitem/collection/RAS/id/1309.

80. http://libcdm1.uncg.edu/cdm/singleitem/collection/RAS/id/317/rec/12.

81. http://libcdm1.uncg.edu/cdm/singleitem/collection/RAS/id/31/rec/13.

82. http://libcdm1.uncg.edu/cdm/singleitem/collection/RAS/id/152/rec/28.

83. http://libcdm1.uncg.edu/cdm/singleitem/collection/RAS/id/1096/rec/14.

84. http://libcdm1.uncg.edu/cdm/singleitem/collection/RAS/id/2002/rec/12.

85. http://libcdm1.uncg.edu/cdm/singleitem/collection/RAS/id/820/rec/10.

Chapter 5

86. Cecelski, *The Waterman's Song*, 121, 126, 130, 138–39, who cites William H. Robinson, *From Log Cabin to the Pulpit; or, Fifteen Years in Slavery*, 3rd ed. (Eau Claire, WI: James H. Tift, 1913), 13.

87. General information on Quakers and slavery comes from Hamm, *Quakers in America*, and Hinshaw, *Carolina Quaker Experience*.

88. Coffin, *Early Settlement*, 221.
89. Hinshaw, *Carolina Quaker Experience*, 132.
90. Newlin, *Friends "at the Spring,"* 78.
91. Browning, *Remembering Old Jamestown*, 9.
92. Ibid., 9.
93. Damon D. Hickey, "'Let Not Thy Left Hand Know': The Unification of George C. Mendenhall," *The Southern Friend: Journal of the North Carolina Friends Historical Society* (Spring 1981): 4.
94. Ibid., 5, 7.
95. Ibid., 5.
96. Ibid., 7.
97. Ibid., 8.
98. Ibid., 9.
99. Ibid., 11.
100. Ibid., 15.
101. Franklin and Moss, *From Slavery to Freedom*, 151.
102. Hickey, "Let Not Thy Left Hand Know," 14.
103. Strong, "Records Tell of Freeing Guilford Slaves."
104. Ibid.
105. Hickey, "Let Not Thy Left Hand Know," 19
106. Ibid.
107. Troxler and Vincent, *Shuttle & Plow*, 232.
108. Ibid., 232–36; for a more sympathetic and slightly different version of this story, see Newlin, *Friends "at the Spring,"* 76–78.
109. Information taken from Coffin, *Reminiscences*.
110. Ibid., 12–13.
111. Ibid., 21.
112. Ibid., 60.
113. Ibid., 107.
114. Ibid., 34, 60.
115. Ibid., 454–55.
116. Ibid., 596.
117. Coffin, *Life and Travels*, 19.
118. Ibid., 20–21.
119. Ibid., 21.
120. Ibid., 45.
121. Ibid., 46.
122. Ibid., 125.
123. Ibid., 128–29.

Chapter 6

124. Khan, *William Still*, 11.

125. Ibid., 15.

126. Still, *Underground Railroad*, xvi.

127. Ibid., xvii.

128. Khan, *William Still*, 17.

129. Ibid., 15.

130. Still, *Underground Railroad*, vi.

131. Ashe and Weeks, *Biographical History*, 473–74.

132. Laurie A. Rolfini, "History's People: Chester County's Passmore Williamson famed abolitionist," *Westchester (PA) Daily Local News*, accessed on 10/25/2014, via http://www.dailylocal.com/lifestyle/20130926/historys-people-chester-countys-passmore-williamson-famed-abolitionist.

133. Still, *Underground Railroad*, 89.

134. Ibid., 89.

135. Ibid., 88–97.

136. Ibid., 129; Still, *Underground Railroad* (1968), 129–30.

137. https://archive.org/stream/johnbranch17821801hayw#page/2/mode/2up. Internet Archive Webpage (accessed 10/03/2014).

138. Ashe, *Biographical History*, 95.

139. Mariah Parker, "Thomas Garrett", from the website "Quakers and Slavery", Accessed 10/25/2014, via http://trilogy.brynmawr.edu/speccoll/quakersandslavery/commentary/people/garrett.php

140. Still, *Underground Railroad, Rev. Ed.*, 129–31.

141. Ibid., 152.

142. Cecelski, *Fire of Freedom*, 14.

143. Still, *The Underground Railroad* (1968), 151.

144. Cecelski, *Fire of Freedom*, 14.

145. Ibid., 13.

146. Still, *Underground Railroad* (1968), 150–52.

147. Still, *The Underground Railroad, Rev. Ed.*, 234, 379–82.

148. Ibid., 424.

149. Ibid.

150. Ibid., 424–25.

151. Ibid., 516.

152. Ibid., 473.

Chapter 7

153. Bearse, *Reminiscences*, 8.
154. Ibid., 9.
155. Ibid.
156. Ibid., 10.
157. Ibid., 10–12.
158. Ibid., 31.
159. Ibid., 34–35.
160. Ibid., 36.
161. Ibid.
162. Calarco, *People of the Underground Railroad*, 16–17.
163. Ibid., 17.
164. Ibid.
165. Ibid., 210.
166. Mitchell, *Underground Railroad*, 19–20.
167. Ibid., 26.
168. Ibid., 26–27.
169. Calarco, *People of the Underground Railroad*, 211.
170. Mitchell, *Underground Railroad*, 31.
171. Ibid., 45.
172. Calarco, *People of the Underground Railroad*, 211.
173. Ibid.

Chapter 8

174. Yellin, *Harriet Jacobs*, 4.
175. Fox-Genovese, *Within the Plantation Household*, 374.
176. Yellin, *Harriet Jacobs*, xix–xx.
177. Jacobs, *Life of a Slave Girl*, 11, 14.
178. Ibid., 11.
179. Ibid., 12.
180. Ibid., 20–21.
181. Ibid., 14.
182. Ibid., 15.
183. Ibid., 18–19.
184. Ibid., 31, 60–61.
185. Ibid., 32.

186. Ibid., 84
187. Ibid., 87–88.
188. Ibid., 89, 92.
189. Ibid., 117.
190. Ibid., 119.
191. Ibid., 147.
192. Ibid., 148.
193. Ibid., 150, 153.
194. Ibid., 154–55.
195. Ibid., 159.
196. Ibid., 161, 163.
197. Ibid., 170–73.
198. Ibid., 227–29.
199. Ibid., 231–33.
200. Ibid., 234–38.
201. Ibid., 241.
202. Ibid., 303.

Chapter 9

203. Siebert, *Underground Railroad*, 11.
204. See the video "Was Mendenhall Plantation an Underground Railroad Station?" http://library.guilford.edu/c.php?g=142981&p=934740.
205. Butler, *Pirates, Privateers and Rebel Raiders*, 206.
206. Hilderman, *Into the Fight Cheering*, 185.
207. See the brochure from a Civil War reenactment in Snow Camp, North Carolina, in the Snow Camp folder, May Memorial Library, Burlington, NC, 5.
208. Browning, *Shifting Loyalties*, 13.
209. Carbone, *Civil War*, 18.
210. Ibid., 33–46.
211. Browning, *Shifting Loyalties*, 68, 77.
212. Ibid., 79.
213. Gould, *Diary of a Contraband*, 15.
214. Ibid., 39.
215. Ibid., 29.
216. Carbone, *Civil War*, 69.

217. Ibid., 116.
218. Click, *Time Full of Trial*, 10–11.
219. Ibid., 10, 32–33.
220. Mobley, *James City.*
221. Ibid., 5–6, quoted in Vincent Colyer, *Report of the Services Rendered by the Freed People to the United States Army, in North Carolina, in the Spring of 1862, After the Battle of New Bern* (New York: Vincent Colyer, 1864), 33.
222. Browning, *Shifting Loyalties*, 107.
223. Ibid., 120.

BIBLIOGRAPHY

Digital Collections

North Carolina Runaway Slave Advertisements, 1751–1840, University of North Carolina–Greensboro. http://libcdm1.uncg.edu/cdm/landingpage/collection/RAS.

"Slavery as We've Heard It," Greensboro Historical Museum. http://archives.greensborohistory.org/digital/slavery.

Books and Articles

Allen, J. Timothy. *Snow Camp, North Carolina*. Charleston and London: History Press, 2013.

Ashe, Samuel. *Biographical History of North Carolina, From Colonial Times to the Present*. Vol. 6. Greensboro, NC: Charles L. Van Noppen Publisher, 1908.

Ashe, Samuel, and Stephen B. Weeks. *Biographical History of North Carolina, from Colonial Times to the Present*. Vol. 7. Greensboro, NC: Charles L. Van Noppen, Publisher, 1908.

Bassett, John Spencer. *Anti-Slavery Leaders of North Carolina*. Baltimore, MD: The Johns Hopkins Press, 1898

Beal, M. Gertrude. *The Southern Friend: Journal of the North Carolina Friends Historical Society* 2, no. 1 (Spring 1980).

Bearse, Austin. *Reminiscences of Fugitive Slave Law Days in Boston*. Boston: Printed by Warren Richardson, 1880.

Boles, John B. *Black Southerners, 1619–1869*. Lexington: University Press of Kentucky, 1984.

Bordewich, Fergus M. *Bound for Canaan: The Underground Railroad and the War for the Soul of America*. New York: Amistad, 2005.

Browning, Judkin. *Shifting Loyalties: The Union Occupation of Eastern North Carolina*. Chapel Hill: University of North Carolina Press, 2011.

Browning, Mary A. *Remembering Old Jamestown: A Look Back at the Other South*. Charleston, SC: The History Press, 2008.

Butler, Lindley S. *Pirates, Privateers and Rebel Raiders of the Carolina Coast*. Chapel Hill: University of North Carolina Press, 2000.

Calarco, Tom. *People of the Underground Railroad: A Biographical Dictionary*. Westport, CT: Greenwood Press, 2008.

————. *The Search for the Underground Railroad in Upstate New York*. Charleston, SC: The History Press, 2014.

Carbone, John S. *The Civil War in Coastal North Carolina*. Raleigh: Office of Archives and History, North Carolina Department of Cultural Resources, 2001.

Cecelski, David. *The Fire of Freedom*. Chapel Hill: University of North Carolina Press, 2012.

————. *The Waterman's Song: Slavery and Freedom in Maritime North Carolina*. Chapel Hill: University of North Carolina Press, 2001.

Chernow, Ron. *Washington: A Life*. New York: Penguin Press, 2010.

Click, Patricia C. *Time Full of Trial: The Roanoke Freedman's Colony, 1862–1867*. Chapel Hill: University of North Carolina Press, 2001.

Clinton, Catherine. *Harriet Tubman: The Road to Freedom*. New York: Back Bay Books, 2004.

Coffin, Addison. *Early Settlement of Friends in North Carolina: Traditions and Reminiscences by Addison Coffin, 1894*. Greensboro: North Carolina Friends Historical Society, 1952.

————. *Life and Travels of Addison Coffin Written by Himself*. Cleveland, OH: William G. Hubbard, 1897. Retrieved from https://books.google.com/books?id=9ZMJKMXqjM4C&printsec=frontcover&dq=inauthor:%22Addison+Coffin%22&hl=en&sa=X&ei=wVc1VLeJLcibyATm3oHwBA&ved=0CDIQ6AEwAA#v=onepage&q&f=false.

Coffin, Levi. *Reminiscences of Levi Coffin, the Reputed President of the Underground Railroad; Being a Brief History of the Labors of a Lifetime in Behalf of the Slave, with the Stories of Numerous Fugitives, Who Gained Their Freedom Through His Instrumentality, and Many Other Incidents*. 2nd ed. Cincinnati: Robert Clarke & Co., 1880. Electronic edition, University of North Carolina Chapel Hill, 2001.

Crow, Jeffery J. *The Black Experience in Revolutionary North Carolina*. Raleigh: Division of Archives and History North Carolina Department of Cultural Resources, 1977.

Crow, Jeffery J., Paul D. Escott and Flora J. Hatley. *A History of African Americans in North Carolina*. Rev. ed. Raleigh: Office of Archives and History, North Carolina Department of Cultural Resources, 2002.

Fox-Genovese, Elizabeth. *Within the Plantation Household: Black and White Women of the Old South*. Chapel Hill: University of North Carolina Press, 1988.

Franklin, John Hope. *The Free Negro in North Carolina, 1790–1860*. Chapel Hill: University of North Carolina Press, 1943, 1971, 1995.

Franklin, John Hope, and Alfred A. Moss Jr. *From Slavery to Freedom: A History of African Americans*. New York: McGraw-Hill, 1994.

Gara, Larry. *The Liberty Line: The Legend of the Underground Railroad*. Louisville: University of Kentucky Press, 1961, 1996.

Genovese, Eugene D. *Roll, Jordan, Roll: The World the Slaves Made*. New York: Vintage Books, 1976.

Gould, William B., IV. *Diary of a Contraband: The Civil War Passage of a Black Sailor*. Stanford, CA: Stanford University Press, 2002.

Hamm, Thomas D. *The Quakers in America*. New York: Columbia University Press, 2003.

Hickey, Damon D. "'Let Not Thy Left Hand Know': The Unification of George C. Mendenhall." *The Southern Friend: Journal of the North Carolina Friends Historical Society* 3, no. 1 (Spring 1981).

Hilderman, Walter C., III. *They Went Into the Fight Cheering: Confederate Conscription in North Carolina*. Boone, NC: Parkway Publishers, 2005.

Hilty, Hiram H. *By Land and By Sea: Quakers Confront Slavery and its Aftermath in North Carolina*. Greensboro: North Carolina Friends Historical Society and North Carolina Yearly Meeting of Friends, 1997.

Hinshaw, Seth B. *The Carolina Quaker Experience, 1665–1985: An Interpretation*. Greensboro, NC: North Carolina Yearly Meeting and North Carolina Friends Historical Society, 1984.

Jacobs, Harriet (writing as Brent, Linda), and L. Maria Child, editor. *Incidents in the Life of a Slave Girl*. Boston: Published by the author, 1861.

Khan, Lurey. *William Still and the Underground Railroad: Fugitive Slaves and Family Ties*. New York: iUniverse, Inc., 2010.

Lefler, Hugh T. *North Carolina History Told by Contemporaries*. Chapel Hill: University of North Carolina Press, 1934, 1965.

McDougall, Marion Gleason. *Fugitive Slaves, 1619–1865*. Boston: Ginn & Company, 1891.

Middlekauff, Robert. *The Glorious Cause: The American Revolution, 1763–1789.* New York: Oxford University Press, 1982.

Mitchell, William M. *The Underground Railroad, from Slavery to Freedom.* London: William Tweedie, 1860.

Mobley, Joe A. *James City: A Black Community in North Carolina 1863–1900.* Raleigh: North Carolina Department of Cultural Resources Division of Archives and History, 1981.

Monk, Linda R. *The Words We Live By: Your Annotated Guide to the Constitution.* New York: Hyperion, 2003.

Newlin, Algie I. *Friends "at the Spring": A History of Spring Friends Meeting.* Greensboro: North Carolina Friends Historical Society, North Carolina Yearly Meeting, Spring Meeting, 1984.

Parker, Freddie L. *Running for Freedom: Slave Runaways in North Carolina, 1775–1840.* New York: Garland Publishing, Inc., 1993.

———, ed. *Stealing a Little Freedom: Advertisements for Slave Runaways in North Carolina, 1791–1840.* New York: Garland Publishing, Inc., 1994.

Parker, Maria. "Thomas Garrett", from the website "Quakers and Slavery", Accessed 10/25/2014, via http://trilogy.brynmawr.edu/speccoll/ quakersandslavery/commentary/people/garrett.php.

Powell, William S. *North Carolina Through Four Centuries.* Chapel Hill: University of North Carolina Press, 1989.

Ready, Milton. *The Tarheel State: A History of North Carolina.* Columbia: University of South Carolina Press, 2005.

Rolfini, Laurie A. "History's People: Chester County's Passmore Williamson famed abolitionist." Daily Local News West Chester, PA. Accessed on 10/25/2014, via http://www.dailylocal.com/lifestyle/20130926/ historys-people-chester-countys-passmore-williamson-famed-abolitionist.

Sherburne, Michelle Arnosky. *Abolition and the Underground Railroad in Vermont.* Charleston, SC: The History Press, 2013.

Siebert, William H. *The Underground Railroad: From Slavery to Freedom, A Comprehensive History.* New York: Macmillan Co, 1898.

Stashower, Daniel. *The Hour of Peril: The Secret Plot to Murder Lincoln before the Civil War.* New York: Minotaur Books, 2013.

Still, William. *The Underground Railroad: Authentic Narratives and First-Hand Accounts.* Mineola, NY: Dover Publications, Inc., 2007.

———. *The Underground Railroad.* New York: Arno Press and the New York Times, 1968.

———. *The Underground Railroad. A Record of Facts, Authentic Narratives, Letters, etc., Narrating the Hardships, Hairbreadth Escapes, and Death Struggles of the Slaves in Their Efforts for Freedom, as Related by Themselves and Others, or Witnessed by the Author*. Philadelphia: William Still Publisher, 1886.

————. *The Underground Railroad. Revised Edition, A Record of Facts, Authentic Narratives, Letters, etc., Narrating the Hardships, Hairbreadth Escapes, and Death Struggles of the Slaves in their efforts for Freedom, as Related by Themselves and Others, or Witnessed by the Author*. Philadelphia: William Still Publisher, 1886.

Strong, Russell A. "Records Tell of Freeing Guilford Slaves." *Greensboro Daily News*, August 6, 1975.

Thurman, Howard. *Deep River and the Negro Spiritual Speaks of Life and Death*. Richmond, IN: Friends United Press, 1990.

Tobin, Jacqueline L. and Raymond G. Dobard. *Hidden in Plain View: A Secret Story of Quilts and the Underground Railroad*. New York: Anchor Books, 2000.

Troxler, Carole Watterson, and William Murray Vincent. *Shuttle & Plow: A History of Alamance County, North Carolina*. Alamance County, NC: Alamance County Historical Association Inc., 1999.

Van Horne-Lane, Janice. *Safe Houses and the Underground Railroad in East Central Ohio*. Charleston, SC: The History Press, 2010.

Velsor, Kathleen G. *The Underground Railroad on Long Island: Friends in Freedom*. Charleston, SC: The History Press, 2013.

Weeks, Stephen B. *Southern Quakers and Slavery: A Study in Institutional History*. Baltimore, MD: Johns Hopkins Press, 1896.

Yellin, Jean Fagan. *Harriet Jacobs, A Life*. New York: Basic Civitas Books, 2004.

INDEX

ABOUT THE AUTHORS

Steve M. Miller is an adjunct history instructor at Forsyth Technical Community College in Winston-Salem, North Carolina, and Randolph Community College in Asheboro, North Carolina. He is also an adjunct ESoL instructor at Randolph Community College. While this is his first effort on a book, Steve wrote a one-act play in 2009, titled *The Gathering*, which was performed at Central United Methodist Church in Asheboro in April 2010. In 2013, he authored an article for issue 37 of *Asheboro Magazine*, "North Carolina's Year of Three Governors," which related the history of the three governors who served North Carolina in 1865.

Steve's career includes over thirty years in manufacturing, with twenty-four of those years in quality management, before he began teaching in 2009. He earned a bachelor of general studies from Indiana University's School of Continuing Studies in 2009. He followed that in 2011 with a master of arts in history, with honors, from American Public University.

He is a native North Carolinian and has resided in Asheboro and Randolph County his entire life. Steve is married and has one son, a daughter-in-law and one granddaughter, on whom he dotes shamelessly.

J. Timothy Allen is a professor of humanities at Strayer University, where he teaches history, religion and humanities. Previously, he taught history and religion in the North Carolina Community College system. An avid writer, Tim has published devotional books (*Seasons in the*

Year; *When the Season Is Dry*; *Mothers Around the Manger*) and *A Theology of God-Talk: The Language of the Heart*. Lately, he has written *North Carolina Quakers: Spring Friends Meeting* (Arcadia Publishing) and *Snow Camp, North Carolina* (The History Press). He has also published academic and popular articles in journals and magazines.

Tim earned a bachelor of arts in religious studies from the University of South Carolina–Columbia; a master of divinity from Southeastern Baptist Theological Seminary; a master of arts in religious studies from the University of North Carolina–Chapel Hill; and a PhD in theological studies from the Graduate Theological Foundation. He and his wife live on a small horse farm in Snow Camp in Alamance County.